The Way of the Desert Elders

Praise for *The Way of the Desert Elders*

"A good part of our modern malaise owes to our forgetting the great wisdom to be gained from the faithful who came before us. What is most compelling about the desert elders is not their saintliness, but rather that their virtue was so often hard-won—as is our own. Their ways can help us along our way too, if only we will avail ourselves of their examples. *The Way of the Desert Elders* serves up their wisdom eloquently, compellingly, and generously."

—**Karen Swallow Prior**, author of *On Reading Well: Finding the Good Life Through Great Books*

"The desert mothers and fathers offer spiritual wisdom that every contemplative should read and ponder. Lisa Colón DeLay offers us a lively and thoughtful guide to several of these ancient mystics through the lens of the seven deadly sins. DeLay invites the reader to identify these universal human patterns within ourselves. She then offers rich practices that are antidotes to open the door to genuine transformation. Highly recommended for serious spiritual seekers."

—**Christine Valters Paintner**, PhD, REACE, author of *Desert Fathers and Mothers* and more than twenty books on contemplative practice

"*The Way of the Desert Elders* is a fascinating exploration of a rigorous Christianity that flourished in the early centuries of the faith. In an era when the practice of Western Christianity is often lax and uninspired, Lisa Colón DeLay brings us spiritual wisdom from our desert mothers and fathers—a hard-won wisdom that has the potential to revitalize contemporary Christianity."

—**Brian Zahnd**, author of *The Wood Between the Worlds: A Poetic Theology of the Cross*

"*The Way of the Desert Elders* is a treasure trove of wisdom. Lisa Colón DeLay expertly introduces and translates the timeless wisdom of the desert ammas and abbas for the present moment. Though I am familiar with the elders, I was continually stunned by the depth of DeLay's insights and applications—a depth rarely seen. If you seek to become more like Christ, read this book carefully and apply what you learn. DeLay and the elders serve as trustworthy guides and are among our great cloud of witnesses. Then be sure to let others know about this book. It is worth much more than its weight in gold. Moreover, the wisdom within it is priceless."

—**Marlena Graves**, author of *Bearing God* and assistant professor of spiritual formation at Northeastern Seminary on the campus of Roberts Wesleyan University

"*The Way of the Desert Elders* is a luminous guide to ancient wisdom for modern souls. With warmth and clarity, Lisa Colón DeLay revives the voices of the desert mothers and fathers, inviting us into a spirituality that is earthy, honest, and deeply healing. A beautiful companion for those seeking transformation in a noisy world."

—**Chuck DeGroat**, therapist, professor of counseling and Christian spirituality, and author of *Healing What's Within*

"The desert ascetics had keen insight into the human spirit and the choices that lead us away or toward the Divine. I appreciate the way Lisa Colón DeLay gifts us with chapters that identify a vice, and then moves into the 'medicine' that the ammas and abbas suggest for the vice to become a virtue. She then explores some of the teachings of Evagrius on growth into holiness and shares some desert practices that we can incorporate into our lives today. I love the earthy humor she brings to these ancient texts, gently weaving in relevance to our lives. This is a great source for spiritual formation."

—**Laura Swan**, OSB, author of *The Forgotten Desert Mothers*

"If you have found yourself wandering in the wilderness of faith over the last few years, *The Way of the Desert Elders* will meet you there and point you to ancient wisdom that will move your faith from your head and heart into your body. Through the stories of these desert abbas and ammas, Lisa Colón DeLay offers thoughtful questions for self-reflection without shame, and simple rhythms to shape your life in the way of Christ. If you're looking for a new way to embody your beliefs, let these elders guide you—to yourself and to a fuller, freer faith."

—**Kate Boyd**, author of *An Untidy Faith: Journeying Back to the Joy of Following Jesus*, founder of The Remembered Table, and creator of the Threaded Bible studies

The Way of the Desert Elders

How the Wisdom of Ancient Christians Sustains Us Today

LISA COLÓN DELAY

Broadleaf Books
Minneapolis

THE WAY OF THE DESERT ELDERS
How the Wisdom of Ancient Christians Sustains Us Today

31 30 29 28 27 26 25 1 2 3 4 5 6 7 8 9

Library of Congress Control Number: 2025022594 (print)

Cover design: Alisha Lofgren & Studio Gearbox
Cover image: Blossoming Heart of Praise by Kreg Yingst / Watercolor Abstract Lanscape by Pobytov; Getty Images and Digital Vision Vectors

Print ISBN: 979-8-8898-3531-8
eBook ISBN: 979-8-8898-3532-5

Printed in China.

I dedicate this work to our spiritual forebears, especially the many spiritual mothers lost to history. Though your names may be forgotten, your legacy lives on in us.

CONTENTS

Introduction 1

Part I: Body

1. Antony and the Beasts: Gluttony to Temperance 17

2. There's Something About Mary: Lust to Purity 35

3. Ladies of the Realm: Avarice to Generosity 59

Part II: Mind

4. Moses the Strong: Wrath to Meekness 83

5 Wee Abba John: Acedia to Faithfulness 105

6. Antony's Successor: Despondency to Hope 119

Part III: Spirit

7. Pillars of the Community: Vainglory to Modesty 135

8. A Twist of Spite: Envy to Celebration 153

9. The Final Delusion: Pride to Humility 167

Part IV: The Ways of the Desert

10. Intimacy with God: Toward Preventive Spiritual Medicine 183

11. Keeping the Elders Close: A Rule of Life 197

Author's Note 217
Resources 219
Acknowledgments 223
Notes 225

Introduction

> For where the soul feeds, there is it nourished, either from the world, or from the Spirit of God.
>
> —Abba Macarius the Great (300–390 CE)

Long ago, large numbers of people abruptly fled the bustling cities and towns of the Roman Empire to live in the barren, uninhabited desert. With no conveniences of civilization surrounding them, hundreds of thousands of men and women chose places of desolation to pursue their Christian spirituality in a unique way. For the rest of their lives. Can you imagine?

These spiritual seekers lived in places that took days to walk to as they began new lives far from the trappings of metropolis or village life. They took shelter in little handmade huts or in caves near *wadis*—dry river valleys where some plants grow because of flooding during heavy rains. Their lives of self-denial and austerity consisted largely of solitude, scripture, and prayer. Who they were, why they did it, and what they can teach us now are the focus of this book.

Many people have never heard of this time in history, known as the desert era, nor of the ascetics who defined it, known as the desert ammas and abbas. My own interest in these desert people began in graduate school as I earned my master's degree in spiritual formation and learned of this era of renewed devotion. How enthralling was the idea that so many people left everything behind to seek intimacy with God in forsaken places. How different from our own lives of constant noise and activity. I realized they had a lot to teach me.

These solitary people didn't survive all alone; most of them also enjoyed worship in communities weekly and had the regular guidance of a spiritual mother or father to sustain them. Their communities laid the groundwork for a massive societal trend. We can think of these desert dwellers as *proto-monastics*, who pioneered religious monastic living. By the fifteenth century, more than twenty thousand Christian monasteries existed throughout areas of Western Europe alone. Many thousands of people throughout the world still enter into this kind of religious community life. The wisdom these spiritual ancestors offer us will unfold soon.

When I published my first book on spiritual formation, *The Wild Land Within*, I wrote about the wise desert hermit of Egypt named Evagrius. I told how his wisdom of the eight afflicting thoughts can remind us of weather systems that come and go in our interior landscape. He was such a compelling figure that I became inspired to write an entire book not just on his life and wisdom but on many of the other forgotten wise men and women of that time.

Usually books about the ancient desert Christians offer short stories of their lives and a collection of their wisdom sayings. This book is different. In these pages, each chapter features one or more of the spiritual mothers or fathers in some depth, with an emphasis on an age-old vice with which they struggled and the contrasting virtue they developed. You might be somewhat familiar with the seven deadly sins, but now you will learn their fascinating desert origins. In contrast, the desert elders' way of seeing the world does not focus on moral failings like deadly sins, but on acquiring deeper understanding of ourselves and nurturing intimacy with God. This perspective is a gift of desert spirituality that will richly bless you in your spiritual growth.

At the end of each chapter, I will invite you to absorb it all more deeply as you reflect on and respond to several questions, as well as pray a prayer in the company of the desert elders. The back of the book has plenty of important extras to guide you as well—don't miss those.

In this book you will find not just a collection of ancient people and tales of temptations written for its own sake. No. I write of the elders to connect them with you, personally, and to nurture spiritual transformation. Your experience will be most beneficial if you can keep track of what hits you deeply as you read along. For that reason, you may want to keep notes in a journal, make notes in the margins, or use a highlighter so you can revisit portions later. Notice, too, which vices or temptations are particularly problematic for you, and which virtues attract you most.

Also, consider these pages as a place to find a particular elder, a desert mother or father, you can pick as your special guide. Just as seekers did in the desert times, you can find a desert elder, or two, with whom you feel a kinship or who struggled with the same struggles that you do now. They can help you move toward virtues and sustain you in greater peace.

Additional material online will help you find more personalized instruction from the wise elder you pick. (See the Resources section at end of the book for the link.) The notes you keep, starting now, will be even more helpful later as we integrate desert spirituality into our context in concrete ways.

A Colorful Cast of Characters

Though it started with a few exiles in the late 200s CE, some of whom were escaping direct religious persecution, the movement grew to a steady stream of people arriving as they searched for deeper spiritual meaning. By the 400s, the exiles numbered well into the tens of thousands, and many travelers and temporary visitors joined them for periods of time as well.

This early period of Christian history, 300–600 CE generally, became a full-blown historical movement as communities of Christians lived as religious *ascetics*. The word *ascetic* comes from the Greek word for strenuous athletic training that involves discipline and deprivation: *askesis*. In a similar sense, these desert-dwellers were athletes, training not for sports or games but for the spiritual contests of life: challenges that involved the totality of themselves. They purged their lives of everything superfluous and turned toward obtaining spiritual victories, which don't come easily.

At the height of the desert movement, a staggering half a million people lived in this way. They made their homes mainly in the barren areas of Egypt, Syria, Arabia, and Palestine. Many lived along places in the unpopulated Nile River Valley and Delta regions, primarily in three desert areas in northern Egypt. And lest we forget, devoted people continued living this way, in these same places, following the desert era—and several hundred still do, right into our time. There they live faithfully, choosing what is genuine over what is expedient.

In Eastern Orthodox Christianity and Oriental Orthodox Christian Churches, many of the desert elders are remembered and honored with their own feast days. (See the Author's Note at the end of this book for an explanation of the distinctions between Eastern Orthodox and Oriental Orthodox.) Many of these elders are included in liturgies still today.

Sadly, many of us living in the West or the United States are unfamiliar with this period in history and these desert Christians. Most are unfamiliar with the biographies of these wise elders, especially the many women who lived in the desert. Most people are stunned to learn that in some desert communities in Egypt at the time, women outnumbered the men by double. Though the elder's lives were quite different from ours, these Christians, who voluntarily chose desert exile, lived out a kind of spirituality that can beautifully inform our own.

Those with a passing knowledge of the desert ascetics may suppose they were some sort of super saints or perfected hermits: pious followers of strict religious rules who had purged themselves of all fleshly desire and pleasure. That is incorrect. They comprise a colorful collection of spiritual seekers and the wise desert elders we call the desert mothers (ammas) and fathers (abbas). And when I say "colorful," I mean it: Among their number were a lively array of people that came in various sizes, shapes, and colors; and some were not just hermits, but hooligans or "harlots" prior to their transformations. Their stories may disrupt our notions of what we think of as "saintly."

These desert dwellers were often bedeviled. They were discombobulated, searching ones—befuddled, bewildered seekers looking for peace and hope, just like many of us are. They battled with their own issues and vices, just as we do. In these pages, as you get to know the seekers who became elders, you'll learn how flawed they were and how earnest. You'll become familiar with their urges, raging emotions, and afflictions, and you will see how they endured longings both human and divine.

That makes their teachings and wisdom even more inspiring and transformative for us, because we struggle in similar ways.

Be aware that some of the anecdotal details of these desert dwellers' lives will test your credulity. Accounts of their lives were first passed through oral tradition and sometimes inscribed many decades after their deaths. They may have gained some embellishments along the way. Try to suspend skepticism as you encounter the stories of the elders. Realize that what is remembered and passed down through generations of spiritual seekers, prior to being recorded in writing, occurred because their lives and wisdom were so influential, admired, and unparalleled. They were worth remembering then, and they are worth remembering now.

So while stories of the desert elders are not always strictly historical, in a modern sense, they are nevertheless important and useful. Offered to you now is a glimpse into their lives and their wisdom. Through them, we can better understand our own longings, struggles, restlessness, and the ordinary desires that come during our spiritual searching.

In a time in which many of us often feel unmoored, the elders can anchor us in our substantial Christian history that includes a desert spirituality to sustain us.

Christians Disillusioned by the Empire's Takeover

The context of the desert era is situated in a period of the change and tumult. It began shortly after a deadly stint of Christian persecution, which was particularly lethal in Egypt. Followers of Jesus were rounded up and tortured. Their churches were burned, and those who didn't renounce their faith were executed.

Emperors Galerius and Diocletian, from 303–311 CE, had up to 3,500 Christians slaughtered.

Then came an incomprehensible reversal. Emperor Constantine saw an opportunity to make the empire great again. At that time, a variety of outside invasions were testing the resilience and cohesion of the Roman Empire. Constantine issued the Edict of Milan in 313 CE, which allowed Christians to worship without fear of persecution. He soon began to merge state and church. He even organized a gathering—which was the first of what would eventually be seven ecumenical religious councils—to homogenize Christian doctrine and develop official creeds delineating Christianity in its particulars. Once it had been infiltrated and shaped by imperial interests, Christianity was protected and eventually privileged. Consequently, what was once a genuine community of faith, emboldened by the blood of faithful Christian martyrs, grew distorted by the power and influence of the ruling upper classes. Wealthy and powerful people began warping Christianity for the aims and benefits of the empire. Arguably, this was the first time Christian nationalism went into effect to benefit an empire—and it has had many incarnations since then.

The Christian community—once loyal to the peasant messiah, Jesus—was rapidly capitulating to empire, institutionally. But some Christians resisted this takeover and responded with a redoubled devotion to the way of Jesus. Some began lives of greater devotion via ascetism and a further commitment to Christian love by caring for the poor, widows, strangers, and sick. And some imitated the lives of the prophets Elijah and John the Baptist, and the master Jesus at the beginning of his ministry, committing themselves to voluntary exile into the wilderness. Hence, with this living martyrdom, the desert movement began.

During the era, the community in the inner desert was called the Cells (Cellia). In this location, each person lived separately in silence with prayer and fasting in their own cell, or small dwelling. Many of the cells were carved out from the rocky landscape, and each dwelling was distant enough from each other that the inhabitants could not see or hear one another. Cells were sometimes grouped in enclaves, with buildings and places of worship beautifully cut out from rock. "Neighborhoods" were made up of solitary hermits living in tiny cell dwellings they made themselves and stayed in during the week. They would meet together weekly.

Solitary living was not for a novice—neither is it these days. Before hermits would seclude themselves in a place like Cellia, they would seek out a spiritual father or mother to train them to adjust to the new rhythms of living. In them were instilled the important ways, practices, values, and habits that occur individually and within a community of people dedicated in this way. Such a pattern for living is also called a *rule of life*. One such place was the large group that gathered in the Nitrian desert area that stretched to the western bank of the Nile River. The other major northern-Egyptian community was called Scete (or Skete), and it was farther away from civilization and considered the utter desert.

In other cases, desert cells were made as small earthen abodes and built closer together. These structures were eventually surrounded with a fortifying wall to keep out marauders. Some in fortified areas constructed long underground tunnels that led to wells or a water source. The Egyptian Abba Pachomius, of Thebes, first codified the guidelines for cenobite (communal) communities. In chapter 3, we will learn some fascinating particulars about what those communities were like.

To this day, some devoted Egyptian Orthodox Christians, also known as Coptic Orthodox Christians, still reside as monastics in community settings in some of these same locations.

Spiritual seekers in the desert setting soon found that even when you leave everything behind, your inner turmoil comes with you. The desert—or any place of solitude, stillness, and silence—soon turns into a proving ground, and a battle ensues. Peace must be found internally. The more experienced elders would always nurture the less experienced. They helped seekers weather these storms as desert spirituality, slowly, became their own.

The Afflicting Thoughts

In his original advice to seekers in the desert, and to his student John Cassian who took this knowledge to the West, Abba Evagrius of Ponticus keenly apprehended and taught that each person who is spiritually searching fights against eight specific "demons." (More on the idea of demons shortly.) Evagrius also called these demons the "eight afflicting thoughts," and they assail us as well. These demons, which we also unpack individually in the coming chapters, are Gluttony, Lust, Avarice, Wrath, Acedia, Despondency, Vainglory, and Pride. In later writings he added the afflicting thought of Envy, which we will unpack in the chapter after Vainglory.

If this afflicting thought list sounds familiar to you, it's because these ideas were later used as a springboard to create a list commonly known now as the seven deadly sins. In each chapter, our desert guides will teach us how we can withstand such temptations and emerge unshackled and victorious.

This book uses words like *demon*, *devil*, *spirit*, and the like, rooted in Evagrius's portrayal of the nine temptations as demons.

This was common language at the time, but the ideas about who—or what—demons were and what they did varied back then, depending on educational and cultural influences. Theories regarding demons have also drastically shifted throughout both Jewish and Christian history. I assure you, this book is not a systematic presentation of demonology!

Though the wise elders held varying opinions of the ontological nature of demons, many considered encounters with them as actual as any kind of physical and material encounter. Some considered the desert a place with demons that abounded and continually tormented spiritual seekers. Some tales describe demon attacks in virtually cartoonish ways, as in the case of Antony the Great, whom we will read about in chapter 1. Other abbas and ammas thought differently about what demons are and what they do. For instance, Abba Loukios, who lived during the fifth century, relates this about demons: "Do not think that a demon is anything other than a human being that has been disturbed by anger and has departed from perception."

When Evagrius wrote about the demons, he spoke about them working in a secondary sense—like parasites. Evil has no *being* in itself, he tells us. Demons only make any effect by taking from what is good. Until now, you may have heard of demons only as fallen angels, an opposing or enemy force, or as diabolical entities. Evagrius conceptualized God as fully sovereign and good, with no equal. To him, demons—though serious—were beatable.

Evagrius teaches that a vice comes about as a habitual perversion of what is good. From a vice comes something *less* than what we are meant for—something that takes us, in a vital sense, to a lesser version of our humanity. To this abba, humans are beings that are susceptible to doing wrong, but are good because they are created inherently bearing the image of Almighty God, who is thoroughly good.

We will learn about all nine afflicting thoughts using a wisdom-based approach, exemplified by Amma Syncletica, who left behind an auspicious life for a monastic life in the fourth century. She cautions, "We must observe the assaults of evil spirits that come from without and also detect the evils within us, which derive from our own thoughts; and we must, in particular, be vigilant towards our thoughts, for they are constantly pressing on us and, without our realizing it, they send us to [an abyss]."

It's important to note that the faith of the desert elders—and their view of humanity, sin, and redemption—is distinct from the version of Christianity that emerged from the influence of the empire. Christianity under the influence of the Roman Empire in the 300s began to combat moral wrongdoing just as you might expect a superpower would do it: within a crime and punishment framework, or as a military tribunal. This remains the most influential framework for wrongdoing in our contemporary context—a pernicious holdover from that time.

The theories of a Western Latin father trained in law and rhetoric, Augustine of Hippo (354–430 CE), also overtook the earlier conceptions of sin held by the church and maintained in the East. Augustine's ideas, which were influenced by the stark dualities present in Neoplatonism, cast a pall on notions of a human's *original blessing* as a created being of God. For many, it ushered in shame as a pivot point in human action. After Evagrius's era, Augustine's perspective about sinfulness helped inaugurate a different notion. It became the adopted doctrine known as *original sin*—a dogma that would have been alien, both in its form and its function, to Jewish Jesus and his Jewish disciples.

This construct of original sin doctrine influences our current Western understandings of sin in many negative ways to this day, and in my opinion, it harms our spiritual understanding and undermines our growth. Augustine held the opposite view of humanity that Evagrius did. Unlike Abba Evagrius and many other desert elders, Augustine contended that humans are totally depraved (intractably corrupt at their core) because, he supposed, ancestral sin is passed down through sexual transmission. By conjecturing that any act of sex happens by sinning, it made every person conceived, therefore, sinful. Thus to Augustine, the first sinful ancestor, Adam, became a literal and metaphorical transmitter of all subsequent human sin—a seminal repercussion. This view was not held widely until the imposition of empire on Christianity. By proliferating original sin doctrine in the empire, it could be asserted that human sin could, and should, be held in check by the empire's assumed "divine authority."

Our spiritual formation is often injured by these misconstrued frameworks, and our theology distorted by it. In this book, we endeavor to re-embrace a pre-empire Christian spirituality, which carries a restored understanding of our humanity and also a better reckoning for how we confront what falls short. While we may be prone to sin and selfishness, as creatures with agency, the image of God in us is never expunged or destroyed.

Take notice: The desert elders did not preside over sins or wrongdoings as though they were crimes. Abba Evagrius said that the one thing necessary in all the spiritual life is to *hear* God. With these spiritual ears, first, we must hear and absorb that we are God's beloved. Second, we must be able to hear when we stray away from the good in order to find restoration and renewal. It is intimacy with God, not punishment, that makes us whole.

Abba Evagrius, a former archbishop once from the highest ranks of the institutional church, wrote that the human interior has certain vulnerabilities. In Greek, "afflicting thought" is the word *logismoi*, which is artfully described by Father Andrew Louth, professor emeritus of Patristic and Byzantine Studies at the University of Durham, as "cracks in the heart."

As you read this book and encounter notions like sin, temptation, demons, and afflicting thoughts, try to remember the way that Evagrius and the elders conceived of human failing. He emphasized the original blessing we retain within us as God's creation, rather than an original sin doctrine that pervaded later times. Remember that the desert elders saw sin not from a crime-and-punishment perspective but as stemming from our vulnerabilities, our "cracks in the heart": susceptibilities that can harm us and others.

Once we learn and name the kinds of cracks we have through this perspective, we can also learn, name, and enact the life-giving virtues that sustain and strengthen us. They transform us into mature and wise people. Such qualities lead us toward a more meaningful, moored, and integrated kind of life. We can then choose a pattern of living that allows for more freedom from worry and fear no matter what is happening around us.

These proto-monastics take temptation and sin very seriously, as we will see in these pages. But, as we face all the afflicting thoughts, this should lead us to wholeness and well-being, not shame and self-flagellation. Through training and faithfulness, and with God's grace, the desert seekers find that dealing directly with their own sins and shortcomings produces spiritual transformation. When living in awareness of what afflicts us, we also begin to live a life without segmentation of the material and the spiritual.

As we continue, the searching and bedeviled seekers and elders walk closely beside us. Complete with their own foibles, insecurities, and struggles, as well as their narratives of hard-won wisdom, they teach us about the external and internal temptations that make faithfulness tricky. We learn too about how virtues can shape us, over time, changing our hearts and reordering our desires to live in ways that sustain us and connect us to others in healthy ways.

Perhaps the first questions to respond to, as we begin, can happen in the margins or in your notebook now. What cracks exist in your heart? In other words, what feels problematic, broken, or vulnerable inside? And what about the elders' lives already inspires you?

Part I
Body

always have God before your eyes wherever you go
ABBA ANTONY

CHAPTER 1

Antony and the Beasts

Gluttony to Temperance

> [The desert elders] have given us all a single goal: to avoid over-eating and the filling of our bellies.
>
> —John Cassian (360–435 CE)

To live as a devout Christian recluse is always an uncommon choice. It certainly was so in the third century. In 271 CE a man named Antony, who would become known as Antony the Great, heard the call from God to give up his considerable wealth and follow Jesus wholeheartedly as a disciple. At first, Antony lived in isolation, just beyond his village. He also sought guidance from a seasoned solitary, Paul of Thebes, who had originally fled to the desert because religious persecution threatened his life. After a stretch of fifteen years, Antony went into deeper solitude for two more decades.

Antony finally emerged in 305 CE because he relented to spiritual seekers who coaxed him out of seclusion to teach them. For years they had pleaded for his guidance, hoping to learn from his teachings how to live simply and faithfully. Abba Antony guided them for five or six years before secluding himself once again. This time was different, however; he saw visitors who came to learn from him, and sometimes he crossed the desert to meet with others.

Countless church communities have honored Saint Antony the Great as a wise spiritual father and celebrate him each year with a special feast day on June 13. What part did this man people called Father of Monks play in a movement that would soon impel innumerable seekers to visit and live in the middle of nowhere?

Most historians and religious scholars agree that Abba Antony's eventual honorific as the Father of Monks came not because he was the first desert ascetic but because of his influence, godly character, and his sunny yet commanding presence, which stood out among other ascetics. One of his contemporaries writes of him: "His doctrine surely was pure and unimpeachable; and his temper is high and heavenly, without cowardice, without gloom, without formality, without self-complacency. Superstition is abject and crouching, it is full of thoughts of guilt; it distrusts God, and dreads the powers of evil. Anthony at least had nothing of this, being full of confidence, divine peace, cheerfulness, and valorousness, be he (as some men may judge) ever so much an enthusiast."

Abba Antony of Egypt stands at the beginning of organized communal living. Later, this lifestyle became more prevalent as the movement of monasticism spread to other regions and, a bit later, throughout medieval Europe where this kind of communal religious life lasted as a societal mainstay for over a thousand years. It's the same kind of vowed life that continues to this day all over the world. Abba Antony wrote some helpful observances for hermitic (solitary) living and cenobite (communal) living as significant situations arose. He was no stranger to struggle. "This is the great work of a human," he writes, "always take the blame for your own sins before God, and expect temptation until your last breath."

Abba Antony is known for his epic battles with demonic spirits. He had terrifying visions and experienced onslaughts of vicious temptations for years. The accounts say that demons even physically attacked and harmed him. Quite a few artists have rendered those horrific assaults in paintings, many of them in the most outrageous and gory depictions imaginable. (If you're brave, do a search for them online.) Less popular, but no less radical, are paintings of Abba Antony doing what he did most: fasting and praying quietly in his cave.

> One should not say that it is impossible to reach a virtuous life; but one should say that it is not easy. Nor do those who have reached it find it easy to maintain.
>
> —Abba Antony the Great

It is said that Athanasius, a church father in Egypt who spent some time in the desert, wrote a chronicle of Antony's extraordinary life, and other contemporaries wrote of him as well. They wrote that early on in Antony's desert experience, witnesses heard all kinds of clamoring from Antony's dwelling and saw many crazed and wild beasts visit his place at night. At one point Antony lay motionless on the ground, having been tortured and wounded almost to death. Villagers found him and carried him to town for treatment, but he begged them to take him back to his desert dwelling.

Once he was back, however, the number of beasts simply increased, and they attacked him again. It sounds like a horror-movie rendition reminiscent of the animal parade going toward Noah's Ark. During the onslaught, Antony finally had a realization. He scolded the demonic beasts, telling them that because none of them could kill him, he knew they were just trying to scare him by their sheer numbers. Very cheeky strategy indeed! Lastly, he stated his resolve: "Here am I, Antony; I flee not from your stripes, for even if you inflict more, nothing will separate me from the love of Christ."

Antony's temptations were lifelong, but those that were physically violent ceased after he frustrated that beastly encounter. He noted that "making the sign of the cross made demons run away." He remained faithful, helpful to others, and jovial. You would think that, after all the terrorizing, he would be traumatized with anxiety and fear, but instead he was refined and softened. It made him humble, patient, and wise, and his students loved him dearly. According to his testimony, all Antony's demonic struggles were eventually subdued by prayer, fasting, and trust in God.

Pleasures of the Table

Long before a horde of beasts tried to rip Antony limb from limb, he encountered temptations involving the life of luxury that he had left behind. These he described as "pleasures of the table." Was Antony a foodie or even a wine snob? I can't tell you for sure. But, for Antony, dining had been sumptuous and frequent; it came with delicious variety. Because of his wealthy family, he ate what he wanted, when he wanted it.

But far away in the desert? Not anymore. Now fasting was a primary practice in his life. When he wasn't fasting, his menu was sparse—usually just bread, water, wild herbs, and salt. These deprivations drove him bananas in the early years. Abba Antony was forthcoming about his struggles with the afflicting thought of this chapter: gluttony.

Being driven to distraction by the thought of food and drink in a way that hinders prayer is what Abba Evagrius calls *gluttony*. Evagrius is the desert elder who first explicated these primary afflicting thoughts, or temptations. He was a person who also came from an affluent and privileged life, he too was familiar with the temptation of gluttony. It was their typical habit, as desert ascetics, to restrict their food intake in the form of fasting to purify their thoughts and direct them to God. Fasting as a practice happened in a variety of ways and was carefully superintended by spiritual mentors.

Abba Evagrius teaches that gluttony, as a primal afflicting thought connected to the body, is not always confined to the overconsumption of food and drink. Gluttony can include the craving for material things—for amassing what culture has told us that we must have and for pleasuring ourselves in indulgent ways. Often we've consciously agreed to participate in gluttony, or maybe we've unwittingly have been swept into its powerful cultural current. Overindulging, which is idol worship, is commonplace. We talk openly about how we binge: on Netflix, candy, sports, energy drinks, shopping, collectibles, coffee, and countless other things. Compulsive gambling can fall into this category of overdoing it. Since the legalization of online sports betting in the United States in 2018, the National Council on Problem Gambling has found that the risk of gambling addiction in the general population increased by 30 percent in just three years, between 2018 and 2021. An estimated seven million people are now affected by this binging behavior.

To live in our culture, replete with abundance, means we often fall prey to gluttony, which includes a variety of overindulgent habits. In this chapter we'll look at several forms of gluttony, as well as a countervailing virtue that can help us work on it, bit by bit.

But first, an important note for those with a history of or current patterns of disordered eating or body hatred: Reading about this may bring up painful personal memories or trauma. If that applies to you, take the liberty to skip these sections and do not imitate the desert fasting ways. Please eat the normal daily caloric intake recommended for you. Seek out alternative practices to fasting from food—some ideas will be provided later in the chapter. We will go into the particulars of why fasting is not strictly about the restriction of food.

Gluttony

In the era of Abba Antony, as well as now, gluttony tends to be associated with urges around food and drink: desiring food or drink so powerfully that we overindulge. A *glut* means an excess, or a surplus. So gluttony is not specifically about a lack of portion control when we eat or drink because gluttony can include any binging behavior.

One way to spot hidden gluttony in ourselves is to stop, reflect, and ask, What do I overdo? What kind of *glut* appears in my day-to-day life? Let's now consider the deeper issues within us, and what we fall prey to, with bouts of gluttony. What internal workings are in play when an attack of gluttony begins?

We all capitulate to or are tempted to gluttony as it relates to the senses of the body or our sensual nature. In other words, all the things inherent in having a material form can incite gluttonous desires—the urge to go too far to please our appetites. Be warned: These are the first things that are tested as we begin to pursue a life of discipline—physical, mental, spiritual, or otherwise. The new limits we levy on our body usually pose direct threats to our habits of bodily pleasure or gratification.

Scientific research affirms that this sensual aspect of gluttony includes an addicting and rewarding rush of the hormone chemical dopamine. There is a deep emotional component attached to this pleasure as well. When it comes to gluttony, we are trying, in a misdirected way, to soothe ourselves. We feel a lack, and we aim to fill it. Consider how normal it is that many of us aim to self-soothe with too much soda, alcohol, salty snacks, sugary treats, or any compulsive and pleasurable behavior.

Any indulgent abundance, including that of food, can obscure what is really happening deep within. The upside, in a spiritual formation sense, is that when we contend with the devil of gluttony head-on, we have an opportunity to learn about relying on God for our strength and provision and not on our misguided efforts.

Food is a basic and primal need, of course. But let's consider that for many of us, it can involve uninhibited luxuriance. Through it we can leverage how we feel pleased or even special. Sometimes food purchases are a way we feel a form of control. Food and drink are typical items we use to reward or enjoy ourselves. We center food in our culture and use it as a means to celebrate and show appreciation, or we may pair up food to painful feelings we cannot express. It's rather easy, in fact, to overly attach to food and drink, and other compulsions, in ways that keep us from maturing spiritually, mentally, and emotionally.

How can we explore the factors underlying our gluttony? By engaging in thoughtful and prayerful reflection, we may end up at the intentional spiritual practice of temperance.

Temperance

To be temperate is to exert moderation and self-restraint. By acting with intentional self-control or employing some brief fasting, we can put our gluttony into check. With temperance, we can push back on our habit of overindulgence. The practice of temperance creates a habit of virtue that counteracts the vice or temptation of gluttony.

The desert ammas and abbas participated in the common ascetic practice of fasting in order to challenge idols, attachments, debilitating crutches, and inordinate loves of food and drink. Oversight by a spiritual mother or father would guide all ascetic practices to make sure they were a good fit, didn't trigger pride, and didn't become disordered. Deprivation is not the *solution* to spiritual issues or bad habits, but it can be one utensil at our disposal—accompanied with wisdom, oversight, and balance—used to tweak our improper attachments. (See the Resources section at the end of this book to find a spiritual director who could guide you if you decide to pursue a fast to confront gluttony.)

Antony learned something we all do when we first devote ourselves to a certain deprivation for spiritual reasons: at first, we can experience a *worsening* of the temptation. The temptations to abandon our goals seem to ratchet up as we begin to confront our compulsions and make spiritual practices like temperance and moderation new features in our lives. Abba Evagrius says that during a fast, the stomach wants to be our master. Make no mistake: During a period of fasting or eating less food, the body protests like it's dying, as if to make one think something terrible is happening, says Abba Evagrius. Our stomach has some demanding expectations and a clock of its own.

When we discipline our life to make room for times of temperance or fasting, we encounter not just our grumpy tummy but conflicts within our schedule, maybe a bad mood, perhaps social pushback, or other barriers. We should expect inward and outward challenges of our resolve as we impose portion control, moderation, or even sweets or alcohol limitations that we aren't used to—and that our friends aren't used to seeing from us. The point of a spiritual practice like fasting is not to prove one has the willpower not to eat, but rather to use the occasion as a vehicle to turn our eyes to God.

A contemporary spiritual elder in the Coptic Orthodox tradition, Mother Lois Farag, writes that the desert elders discovered that lengthy fasts of multiple days actually spurred counterproductive results, like pridefulness at their achievement or binge eating. Hence, she says, the elders often suggested *moderation* instead of abstinence, especially for beginners. All this helped enact the practice of temperance to their lives more generally.

In our context, instead of total food restriction, it may be wiser for us to pick differently. For instance, we could fast by skipping one meal per week or forgoing sweets for a week. When I fast from food, it's usually just once or twice per month. I usually only fast for twenty-four to forty hours without food because the body begins to consume muscle to sustain itself after a few days, and that seems counterproductive to my long-term health. We need to select a wise restriction, hopefully with the help of a trusted spiritual mentor. The desert elders tell us we should always pray for strength to endure. Most of all, we must remember that the power of the resurrected Lord works in and through us to sustain us in our temperance no matter what our temptation—be it to gorge on food or feed some other excessive appetite. There are no prizes for doing a fast. Awareness is the reward we can find through a variety of methods of temperance; and picking a good fit for your needs is most important. Fasting is just one way to encourage temperance. There are many alternatives to withholding all food in a fast. Temperance can also be exercised by abstaining from social media, TV, nonessential shopping, doom scrolling, or video games. These can be just as challenging and are also suitable practices. One can consider refraining from *unhealthy* foods for a set period of time as a spiritual practice; think of "special things" like chocolate, alcohol, candy, foods with processed sugar, caffeine, or tasty junk foods devoid of proper nutrition. Whatever you pick, be sensible and see your temperance practice through to the end.

Nourishment in the Desert

When the devil tempts a fasting and hungry Jesus in the desert, Jesus replies by telling the devil that a person "does not live by bread alone, but by every word that comes from the mouth of God" (Matthew 4:4). Jesus is quoting from the Torah, the Hebrew Scriptures that he would have committed to memory. His words are rooted in Deuteronomy 8:3, which relates to testing and hunger in the desert and offers a story that communicates the provision of God. When God delivered nourishment called manna to the Israelites in the wilderness, God gave them even more than food—it was sustenance for their souls and encouragement for their spirits. Direct support.

The spiritual practices of the desert cultivate this sustenance too. If we stuff our stomachs to try to make ourselves feel better, how can we know the sustaining power of God for our basic fulfillment? We can't get by on such spiritually empty calories.

When we bring some bit of desert austerity into engagement with our lives of gratuitous abundance, we can challenge our unconscious expectations for comfort, pleasure, and appeasement. If we put our food overconsumption to the test, we may find that our meal schedule, our cravings, our comfort foods, or our portion sizes are like little gods, created to serve and please us. These gods can quickly turn the tables on us and rule us instead.

Our ordinary struggles, such as temptations to overindulge, are areas where we can learn the most. These opportunities give us a proving ground to discover what hinders us. We can only speculate on those things if we don't "test the spirits and discern," as the elders tutor us.

For instance, say we skip a meal and use the times we think about food to redirect our attention to pray for and be in solidarity with those who live in a conflict zone and who go hungry. Can this experience teach us something about our wants in relation to the lives of the needy that merely reading about such news cannot? Undoubtably.

When we test our temptations—whether gluttony or any vice introduced in this book—by actively opposing them, our underlying appetites and attachments will surface. That gives us an opportunity to understand them better. Our cravings or tendencies toward self-indulgence are revealed best this way.

When we fast or limit our intake of some substance or indulgent activity, we can see our flawed assumptions more clearly.

What Do We Truly Seek?

Interestingly, John Cassian (360–435 CE), who brought the teachings of Evagrius and the eight afflictions to the West, believed that gluttony arises from lust, or intense desire. Abba Evagrius emphasizes the importance of self-control and moderation—for the body and the mind—urging his fellow ascetics to cultivate a disciplined approach to their desires. He instructs that by truly recognizing the fleeting nature of sensual pleasures, seekers can redirect focus toward the nourishment of their souls and the pursuit of spiritual fulfillment found in prayer and connection with God. As we plan moments to stop to see the bigger picture, we too can be more aware of cultivating a life that brings more satisfying spiritual fulfillment and godly connection.

> He who cherishes his stomach and hopes to overcome the spirit of fornication is like one who tries to put out a fire with oil.
>
> —Abba John Climacus

We live in a culture that valorizes overconsumption and overindulgence of all kinds. Our culture tempts us all to overconsume through things like food festivals, holidays, food-eating contests, and food excess during sporting events and in tv shows to name just a few. Plus, billions of dollars go to food advertising and making processed food literally addicting. So it's understandable that we feel confused or ashamed about our consumption or about food in general.

Given all these messages, we may feel guilty eating (or not eating) and overly anxious about food. These mixed messages make the whole topic exhausting and may induce a kind of paralysis. Even worse, diet culture twists our apprehensions about food and desire into a billions-a-year profit-making machine—reminding us with cunning lies we already half-believe that we've been made less loveable because of our relationship to food. Those messages tell us that excess weight equates to ugliness. Just in time—their new product, prescription, or pill will fix us! Try this new amazing injection, phone app, or a program, they urge. This all takes from the goodness we are meant to enjoy in a life without shame of who we are. With temperance and emotional safety through connection with God, we find a way out of this trap.

To obey the suggestions or pressures of a warped culture, which often pumps or twists gluttony, is to succumb to a painful unexamined life. Our natural desires for food aren't wrong or shameful. It is only our willing consent to overindulge that becomes gluttony and entraps us. Thankfully, we can learn perspectives and time-tested spiritual practices to curb the temptations of gluttony and nurture temperance. Let's consider what would it look like to thoughtfully value our desires and maintain restraint.

The Three Degrees

The practical wisdom of desert elders tells us that eating *differently* can help us grow mindful and avoid gluttony. By eating differently, we learn to realize when we are starting to feel we've had enough nourishment from food. Gregory of Sinai, a Greek monk from Smyrna (c. 1260–1346 CE), gave consumption a lot of thought. He wrote that there are three degrees regarding eating. These degrees are sensed in the body, and we can decide which to abide by *prior* to consuming food or drink. These degrees are temperance, sufficiency, and satiety.

First, what he terms *temperance* happens at mealtime when we stop eating while we're still somewhat hungry. We've had the healthy amount of calories, as it were, but perhaps we crave some more vittles to top ourselves off. Nevertheless, we stop eating; that's temperance. *Sufficiency* is when we eat just enough for normal nourishment and not a bit more. We stop at just the right time. This is more likely to happen if we eat carefully and slowly. *Satiety* occurs when we eat more than enough, and instead of feeling satisfied, we feel full. Abba Gregory suggests that repeatedly moving past the first two to the final one puts one in danger of becoming a habitual glutton. It takes thoughtful practice, but I've personally found his wisdom very useful as I enjoy food but desire to consume mindfully.

For a moment, consider your habits of eating. In which of the three degrees do you find yourself most of the time? And think about some other habit of consumption that does not relate to food. In which of the three degrees do you find often yourself when it comes to that?

When asked about fasting at a time when some ascetics were going to extremes and skipping food for many days, fourth-century Abba Poeman said, "For my part, I think it better that one should eat every day, but only a little, so as to not be satisfied." A number of desert elders repeated this same wisdom to their students. For Abba Poeman, being hungry was not the point. Rather, turning that little pang—of feeling not quite satisfied—into a way to turn to God for ultimate satisfaction served a more beneficial purpose. Abba Antony the Great teaches that self-control is the deepest priority: "Do not trust in your own righteousness; do not worry about the past, but control your tongue and your stomach." He underscores that it's not mainly about the amount of food eaten and when, but about how one maintains control that comes from within. This includes what we want to eat plus what we say.

Regular practices like slowing down and expressing gratitude will help us enjoy and savor our food and drink during our meals. Too often, many of us get into terrible habits of rushing. Our stomachs complain with indigestion. As we take our time, let's also be sure to notice and enjoy the tastes, temperatures, and textures of our experience. Dethroning our gluttony must be centered in temperance, charity, and trust.

Sharing the Grapes

Once upon a time, someone brought a cluster of grapes to Abba Macarius the Younger, who was head of the monastic community. Of course, in the desert, fresh fruit is a rare treat. Though Abba Macarius was delighted to see the gift and would have enjoyed eating the grapes, he decided to abstain. He had the grapes sent to a monk who was ill and who might savor some refreshment.

When *this* brother saw the grapes, he rejoiced. But then he remembered that he was aiming to overcome his gluttony and that this sweet treat was off limits. So he had the grapes sent to a very strict brother who never faltered with his desires for food. He might enjoy the grapes as a very rare treat, guilt-free.

This brother was given the grapes but at the same time he was told about his reputation of self-denial. Because this brother did not want to give in to the temptation of pride—through this special recognition and reward of grapes for his skilled ascetic practice—he had the grapes sent along to another brother.

And so it went, each brother sending the grapes on, as a treat, to someone else, until they finally came back to Abba Macarius, to honor him. When the abba saw the grapes again, he was inspired by the community's self-denial and magnanimity. And just as they had done, he also did not eat the grapes.

This is not a story about how raisins were invented. It's also more than a story about vanquishing gluttony. It's about the kindness of a community. Let's look closely: Here was a place of selfless generosity. The temptation to gorge on a rare sweet treat would have tempted them all. The brothers didn't think of their own appetite first. They did not live from a mentality of scarcity or selfishness. Nobody took the grapes for their own benefit; rather, each endeavored to pass along the treat to someone else to enjoy. In the end, their temperance and their sacrifice, not their consumption, made the biggest impression and a lasting legacy.

Reflect and Respond

- How does gluttony show up in your life?
- In what ways could you test and moderate any problematic attachments to eating, drinking, or other ways of overindulging?
- The story of Abba Macarius and the grapes—of abstaining in deference to others—has stood the test of time over many centuries. How does it speak to you now?

Pray

O Provider, Sustainer, Giver,
Deliver me from gluttony, by your grace.
Give me eyes to see my errors and attach more to you
that you may be ever more my Bread of Life.
Amen.

CHAPTER 2

There's Something About Mary

Lust to Purity

> One must not accept the following two thoughts: fornication and judgment of one's neighbor. When the enemy presents one of these we must rise up and pray; and pray again, with tears to God, and God will deliver us.
>
> —Amma Sarah (408–450 CE)

Sometimes people we admire have fascinating backstories—checkered pasts they lived prior to their lives of devotion. A while ago I met a church lady, my mother's age, who seemed fairly ordinary to me at first—until she told me about her globe-trotting past. She was a glamourous flight attendant living in artsy Greenwich Village of New York City during the vibrant and groovy 1970s. She once went to a Rose Bowl game with a famous astronaut from an Apollo mission. During her many travels for work, she met a drummer in a band. As their relationship ensued, she flew to meet up with him in different cities as the band toured. What happened at those after-parties might be stuck in a purple haze or forgotten by now, but at this point, they've been married for a number of decades. The drummer now puts his professional percussion skills to use in the local church, and she has brought the gospel to countless children as a teacher.

Did you ever start to make assumptions about someone, only to realize that they have an unexpected backstory? Some of the desert seekers, like Mary of Egypt, had unexpected backstories too. She's an elder to remember.

Mary Aegyptica (344–421 CE) was what some people would call "a floozy" with an addictive personality. She is known to some as Mary of Egypt, and to others by the antiquated and disparaging title of "Mary the Harlot." By the time Mary was old enough to know better, but too young to be running off, she left her parents to look for thrills in the big city of Alexandria. Sexually insatiable and with no business savvy, Mary didn't care about getting compensated for her tempting talents.

Just like most of us, Mary was impelled to seek pleasure because meaning and purpose in her life was in short supply. For necessities, she got by with the occasional spinning of flax or panhandling. Mary went through men like some people go through tissues during allergy session. After about seventeen years, she hatched an appalling, secret scheme. It sounds like a plot for a sleezy reality TV series. Her plan was as daring as it was decadent—an adventure that would change everything.

Mary decided to travel all the way from Egypt to Jerusalem along with a group of devoted Christian pilgrims. Mary didn't have any religious interest in this trip, mind you; she relished her plan to sexually seduce as many devout pilgrims as she could who would also foot her bill along the way. She even kicked off her seedy excursion by paying for her boat fare with sexual favors. Mary enjoyed the drama that lust and fornication ignited, and her exploits were many along the trip, which likely lasted ten days or longer.

Everything was going to plan until they all arrived in Jerusalem. There she tried to enter into the Church of the Resurrection for the Feast of the Exaltation of the Holy Cross. But she couldn't. It was like a force field was stopping her entry. She bounced off it three or four times. How bewildered she was to not simply step foot in the building.

Then the truth hit her: She had been horrible to others, herself, and God. Her way of living wasn't living at all. Stung by remorse, she wept bitterly and prayed for forgiveness.

One nun came to Amma Sarah and said to her: "Pray for me, my lady." The blessed one said to her: "Neither will I have mercy on you nor will God unless you have mercy on yourself, fulfilling the virtues as the [Elders] have commanded us."

Mary wanted a fresh start, so she vowed to change immediately. Her life of sex and seduction was over. When she attempted to enter the church this time, she finally could. Perhaps there were uncomfortable moments inside where she recognized all the men she had fornicated with on the trip. (I wonder if everyone exchanged hesitant glances? Awkward.)While she was worshiping, she heard the words, "If you cross the Jordan, you will find glorious rest and true peace." As she left the church, a man gave her three coins, and with them she bought three loaves of bread. This would be the best money she'd ever spent.

Ready to start over, Mary of Egypt crossed the Jordan River on a small boat the next day. She dried out the bread so she could eat a few crumbs at a time, and it supposedly lasted her for years. She spent the rest of her life living off whatever edible plants and herbs she found in the wilderness as she worshiped God and lived a life of purity, repentance, and complete devotion.

But there's more. Before we consider the afflicting thought of this chapter, lust, more thoroughly, let's learn a bit more about Mary's life in the desert. The reason we even know about Mary is its own story worth sharing.

Abba Zosimas Meets Mary

Once upon a time, an elderly monk named Abba Zosimas was off in the wilderness and away from his monastery, which was located near Jerusalem. For twenty days he fasted and prayed. One day he was praying when, out of the corner of his eye, he saw a form so terrifying he was sure it was a demonic apparition. He made the sign of the cross, which calmed him down. Then he realized this willowy form was actually a human. The person had short, shock-white hair and was sunburnt to a crisp.

After weeks of isolation, Abba Zosimas was actually relieved to find some human company. He followed the figure to chat—and weirdly, a bit of a chase ensued. Perplexed, Abba Z called out something like, "Hey there, why all the running?" The figure was Mary, as you probably guessed. However, she was buck naked and looking for cover. Her clothes had worn out and fallen off long before. She never expected to meet anyone so far off in the desert where she was. And, of course, there were no stores around to buy clothing.

Mary sensed her sparse menu of herbs and bread crumbs had made her alarmingly skinny—even terrifying. She broke her silence and having never met the man, Mary said to him, "Forgive me, Abba Zosimas, but I cannot turn and show my face to you. I am a woman, and as you see, I am naked. If you would grant the request of a sinful woman, throw me your cloak so I might cover my body and then I can ask for your blessing."

She knew his name! With his mind fully blown, Abba Z realized he was in the presence of an advanced ascetic—a spiritual mother with extraordinary gifts. He gave her his cloak. Now *he* wanted a blessing from *her*. He was insistent.

With the nakedness situation resolved, a sincere but blundering back-and-forth dialogue happened as they kept asking for blessings of each other. They were both very reverent and self-effacing people, after all. After a bit, Mary not only told Abba Z her whole story but revealed that she had been living as a grazing hermit out in the wilderness for forty-seven years. He was the first person she'd seen in that whole time.

The highlights of the rest of the story include some wonders. (Here, a suspension of skepticism is important.) Abba Z noted that Mary had some levitating powers when she prayed. Furthermore, when the abba saw her again the following year, she crossed the Jordan River by walking on the water, and then crossed back again the same way, after he gave her communion. Full of surprises—that's Mary for you.

The next year, Abba Z found Mary's body. She had passed away and managed to leave behind a note that asked him to bury her. As he contemplated what to do, a lion approached out of nowhere and started licking Mary's feet. Was the lion grieving?

With no shovel for digging a grave, Abba Z saw an opportunity. When asked, the lion obliged Abba Z and used its large paws to dig a resting place for Mary's body.

When he returned to his monastery, Abba Z shared Mary's story, which she had asked him to keep secret until after her death. It was then recorded for posterity. The beloved abba, who was revered by many, lived to be almost a hundred years old. This grazing hermit, Mary Aegyptica, is venerated as a saint in the Eastern and Oriental Orthodox Churches. Her feast day is April 1. I don't think she would mind that such a date would much later be known as April Fool's Day—if she could be counted as a transformed "Holy Fool" for God, I suspect she would accept that moniker gladly and humbly.

So was Mary a skilled cat lady on friendly terms with a local lion? Could she walk on water and levitate? Parts of this story seem farfetched to my modern mind and likely to yours. The stories of elders that include harmonious interactions with animals are also written to remind us that full restoration to our original Edenic lives can happen through reconciliation with God. We are to realize that renovated lives are replete with instances of the shalom of all creation—including being on friendly terms with wild animals. All stories of elders are recorded out of deep reverence and awe. They thoroughly embrace the miraculous and mysterious. And above all, these narratives tell us what people thought of the elders and how much they valued them and admired their devotion and holiness. These were saints they endeavored to imitate.

Lust Is About Taking

As we turn to the afflicting thought of this chapter, it's important to note at the outset that the temptation of lust, and accompanying fornication, are simply this: *desiring* to do what we know is wrong, inappropriate, or indecent. At times, lust isn't related to sex at all. In a certain way, we can lust to exert power or dominance. We can lust for wealth, status, success, or any kind of pleasure. Let's remember this: Lust is about taking.

Writer and Coptic Orthodox Christian Phoebe Farag Mikhail says, "Whether it's sexual lust or lust for power or possessions, in order to fulfill that lust, one often must dehumanize others, whether it's objectifying a person sexually or exploiting people for personal gain." In the process of dehumanizing others we, by consequence, dehumanize ourselves. This is not the life-giving way that gives rise to spiritual maturity. Mary learned this.

In the case of Mary, the grazing hermit, we find an example about how the vice of lust can be transformed. She is the patron saint of penitents, converts, and chastity in some communities. She exemplifies how a life full of afflicting thoughts and damaging actions of lust and fornication can be remade into one of purity.

What Is Purity?

Pure is usually how we describe the condition of something that is not contaminated or polluted. Pure gold has gone through the fires of refinement to be untainted. Pure water has been filtered and decontaminated to be nontoxic. Maintaining purity often requires struggle or difficulty.

In the case of people who choose a life of purity—in Mary's case, a life of sexual abstinence after a time of extreme sexual abandon—we can think of purity as setting oneself aside for a special purpose that is meant for God alone. The stringency of this life of purity isn't the best path for all of us. But, learning more deeply about what purity entails helps us to begin to mature spiritually in new ways that challenge our inaccurate notions about purity.

Generally speaking, living in a state of purity can take on physical or spiritual elements and will vary in expression from person to person. For Mary, purity from the action or consequences of lust and the extreme way she conducted her life were what made her transformation so memorable and, for many over the ages, so inspiring.

It helps to know a bit about Mary's ancient context. We know that in those early Christian centuries, both men and women struggled with lust just as powerfully they do now, yet men and women were not even remotely on equal footing in their society when it came to engaging in sexual activity. Male dominance allowed or even rewarded sexual activity for men and punished it for women. Marriages were arranged by families as business transactions and were not based on individual desires—whether romantic desires or practical ones. Marriages only happened among families within classes and not across classes, but lust could pop up anywhere. There are innumerable instances of powerful people, out of their lustful temptations and habits, taking advantage of and harming the powerless. The enslaved had few legal or human rights, and it was illegal to marry anyone who was free. Many people who were enslaved—both men and women—were exploited sexually by their enslavers.

Enslavers themselves had the option, under the law, to use and misuse their enslaved men and women in whatever ways they wanted to, and they frequently sexually abused them. Sometimes other people would pay enslavers for the opportunity to also sexually assault their enslaved people. Of course, such abuses were also about misusing power, not just about satisfying lustful desire.

Formerly enslaved people, then, sometimes did sex work as a way to survive, having few options to make an income. They were already disadvantaged and economically confined because they were considered undesirable and outcast in Roman society. Hence, they were also not well-protected under the law. This situation was no outlier. Prior to Christian influences, at least 30 percent of the population was enslaved. Many subjects of the empire were non-citizens and shifts to serf-like labor meant that many freed people lived under conditions similar to that of enslavement. Whether free or enslaved, many women and men could never ascend to a higher social position. The confinement and meager life of outcast was Mary of Egypt's reality.

> They said of Amma Sarah that she was attacked greatly by the demon of fornication for fifteen years, and she never prayed to see an easement in this war but only said: "God strengthen me!"

In this period, countless poor people, whose lives and stories are lost to us now, came to the desert with little to lose. They literally escaped their situation. Some people took off for the desert for reasons besides strictly spiritual ones. They might be fleeing forced labor, military duty, debt, or taxes. Some women were fleeing enslavement, prostitution, arranged marriages, or dangerous situations. Escaping to monastic communities to start a new life became a favorable choice for thousands at the time. It meant, however, a new life of sexual abstinence—including not marrying and not having children. Lust tempted many of these ancient Christians, as it would any of us.

Desiring someone or something outside of what is permissible is a common human temptation, and the initial lust feeling itself isn't sinful. It's the choices we make that capitulate to those temptations that create habits of vice that can become areas of bondage that hurt ourselves and others. Habits of lust can even become an addiction.

A Chaste Life

Chastity refers to forgoing sexual activity outside of what is permitted. In our times, this tends to refer to relations outside one's marriage and includes having no sexual relations when one is unmarried. We know that we cannot go without food, a primary impulse, for too long. But plenty of people have lived meaningful and happy lives committed to chastity, even though humans have a natural desire for sexual contact.

Thousands live in communities that take vows of chastity in our time. Christians in Roman Catholic, Anglican, Episcopal, Lutheran, Eastern Orthodox, and Oriental Orthodox churches today have opportunities for monastic life that include vows of chastity. Even non-monastics like priests in the Roman Catholic church are still expected to be celibate; in the Eastern Orthodox, Oriental Orthodox, Anglican, and Eastern Rite Catholic traditions, however, priests are permitted to marry and have children. All of them are expected to defeat desires and temptations of lust. Those committed to living a celibate life often feel it is a special calling given to them to be united to God as a spouse forever in a spiritual marriage. A marriage to anyone else, or anything that would compromise that loyalty, hinders this vow.

> [Just as] the force of the waves batters a ship without ballast in a storm, the thought of fornication will act similarly on the intemperate mind.
>
> —Abba Evagrius

All ascetics of the desert era, like Mary Aegyptica, gave up sexual activity and any sexual pleasures to live in chastity as an act of devotion to God. This happened in a few ways. Some were consecrated virgins—meaning they decided early on to forgo sexual activity for life; some had first lost a spouse through death before they took a vow of chastity; and some left lives full of sexual activity. Some were born free, some were formerly enslaved and likely exploited sexually, and some were escaping enslavement that included sexual exploitation or involvement. In some places, twice as many women as men took refuge in desert communities, likely because it was an appealing alternative to "life as usual" for women living in their contexts, which gave them few options.

Celibate in Disguise

Since a life of chastity meant monastics would not marry and would not have children, there were no marital expectations to contend with in the desert communities. This presented a unique opportunity in disguise—literally. Some women successfully blended into male communities. They did this by wearing men's clothing, staying in solitude, and often keeping a vow of silence. Such women were often assumed, by others, to be eunuchs who could not grow facial hair. Some of these women, like Theodora of Alexandria, Apollinaria, Matrona, and Eugenia, grew renowned for their holiness. For many of those, it was only in their preparation for burial that they were discovered to have been women all long. The desert communities offered women a special kind of refuge because they needn't have concerns about marital or romantic pursuers, or sexual predation.

It's a surprise to no one that sex—this particular aspect of human nature that is vital for the survival of our species and one of our most powerful inherent drives—is one of the trickiest urges to contend with, then and now. History shows us again and again that without certain prohibitions or boundaries on sexual appetite and activities, people and whole societies sink into sexual corruption and chaos that cause harm. And the vulnerable suffer most in cases of sexual exploitation. Honest reflection also shows that the church has often failed in navigating this territory of understanding lust and aspects of our sexuality. Through history, church folks have made a confusing mess in this category and have caused untold harm and suffering at times.

As for lust, things have run amok. Our current society—in the United States but almost everywhere in the world—is saturated with all things titillating and sexual. Stories, songs, movies, adult games, advertisements, and even beauty standards that value women only within a narrow age of fertility and body type are just a few examples. Sexual abstinence is often viewed with disdain, suspicion, or intense ridicule.

Sexual desire unbridled has its price. Especially with the advent of certain technologies, the instances of massive sexual exploitation through human trafficking and the pornography industry are incalculable. The most popular three pornography sites have 5.81 billion visitors each month who stay for an average of eighteen minutes. Those numbers barely account for its use, but even on their own, are staggering. People under twenty-five years old in the United States admit to knowing about sex mainly through their regular exposure to pornography, some as early five or six years old. These performances are not realistic portrayals of sex or helpful ways to learn. They cause harm because, through viewing, people begin to normalize that which is illusory, debasing, and objectifying. They have a pernicious effect on young minds, especially.

Through mass proliferation of pornographic material, many people have their lust inflamed but lack examples of appropriate behavior, healthy communication, trust-building, and learning about agency and sexual consent. Navigating the normal emotions and social interplay of faithful relationships and healthy sexual activity is meant to occur in a setting of loving-kindness and stability. We learn these things through worthy examples with spiritually and emotionally mature education and guidance, not through porn sites that are powered by lust. In our era, we are pressured to believe we need sex-on-demand to live healthy or full lives. But there are millions of examples that prove otherwise, now and through the ages.

Yet in trying to combat lust, some approaches have caused their own spiritually destructive outcomes. Consider the shame-filled sexual abstinence programs prevalent in some churches in recent decades, and purity culture mindsets that hold young women responsible for men who falter with sexual temptations. We are often left to wonder, What is sexually virtuous for a Christian? What does holiness look like outside of vowed monastic celibacy? What is the way to navigate the territory of sex and the afflicting thought demons of lust and fornication?

> Many people who are tempted by pleasures of the flesh do not sin with the body but lust with the mind; they keep their bodily virginity but lust in their heart.
>
> —Gerontius of Petra

I do not write this chapter easily or blithely. I do not write it to offer easy answers. Some Christians choose a life of sexual abstinence, but few would claim it's the only way to follow Jesus faithfully. Though there are a variety of perspectives, I won't make my own often semi-formed opinions the focus of this chapter. Yet I do want us to ask, whether it's about lust or any other afflicting thought, What does Jesus say about it? Let's rely on the Teacher himself to set our boundaries and show us the way.

Jesus's Way Forward

One of the best ways to encounter the hardest questions is to listen carefully to and follow the admonitions of Jesus. If Jesus does not explicitly address some detail of what we are up against, he often covers it in the way he asks us to interact with others and how to treat ourselves.

Some will be disappointed to hear that Jesus equates the sexually betraying *act* of adultery with merely *thinking* lustfully. Adultery is forbidden in Jewish law, and in our time the act is considered legal grounds for dissolving a marriage contract. But the notion that merely thinking lustful thoughts constitutes adultery? That sounds extra. What a high standard for purity Jesus sets when it comes to lust. How can merely dwelling on a thought about a forbidden act be just as bad as doing it?

Let's notice his twist, and the crux of the issue, in his words. In Matthew 5:27–29,

> Jesus says, "You have heard that it was said, 'You shall not commit adultery.' But I say to you that everyone who looks at a woman with lustful intent has already committed adultery with her in his heart. If your right eye causes you to sin, tear it out and throw it away. For it is better that you lose one of your members (like your eye) than that your whole body be thrown into hell."

Here, Jesus teaches about honoring each other. Giving in to lust makes this impossible. He emphasizes that our *intentions* are what lead us into trouble. Jesus, specifically, puts a smack on those who objectify women, fantasize about them, or dwell on their thoughts of sexual gratification with them. He was speaking directly to men at the time, but I imagine some of the women nearby sensed their own lustful mistakes through his admonition too.

Let's again remember that it's not the initial, momentary, lustful temptation at issue—because those situations are hard-wired within us as a species. Jesus tells us that *lingering* on lustful thoughts is just as immoral as doing the lustful things. And what does purity involve? Jesus says that the purity—or chastity—of our mind is what we have at stake with regards to lust. Through his shocking gouge-out-your-eye hyperbole, he invites us to ask, Am I willing to put myself in chains in an abyss for this vice? Where is my focus and where should it be? The distraction of lust takes us to places we shouldn't go.

With lust and fornication, we take something for ourselves. In contrast, intimate love is about *giving* for the benefit of the other and enjoyment together. Lust revolves around selfish intent. Acting out of lustful temptations reveals our acute sense of lack. Rather than stability, there is a vacuum that urges us to think we deserve to be satisfied when and how we desire to be, and it will never be enough.

Whether we carry out illicit desire or we simply give lustful desire a playground in our brains are distinctions with no difference. Either way, Jesus says that lust must be understood as an issue of the interior life. What we give our attention to matters.

Lustful temptation follows a familiar route. It starts as a stirring of tempting thoughts. If we thwart those right away, we can be free. But when lust bites down, the poison from those fangs come as powerful desire that may become lustful arousal. That excitation turns into fantasy, illusion, or planning where, when, or how we will consummate our desire. We may find ourselves willingly doing the demon's work: dabbling in what we know to be wrong or not appropriate. *Because* it is wrong or forbidden is precisely why we are tempted with it.

Healthy Desire?

Some people will want "the measurements" when it comes to navigating lust and fornication. What is exactly wrong or right? Precisely with whom or what is sinful? What is going too far? Sometimes wanting these specifics are how we avoid feeling fully responsible or guilty for our future mistakes. It's part of dallying with temptation. This struggle, however, reveals our part in starting to capitulate. Looking for the loophole means that we are playing with the devil in the details, but a devil all the same.

We are wondering, Can I have it both ways—get the forbidden that I desire and get it without negative consequences?

Let us be challenged about how we feed our lust. When we ingest things like lust-filled television, music, dance, books, movies, images, videos, online or in-person chats, or flirting, such things have a way of ingesting us instead. What *is* possible is that we dare to try to live a *chaste* life—one that maintains, or at least regularly reaffirms, purity. This kind of life extends beyond sexual aspects alone. Desert spirituality gives us a jumping-off point so we can find a way to grapple with the initial lusts that threaten to consume us or harm our relationships.

The desert ammas and abbas, like Mary Aegyptica the grazing hermit, traded what was fleeting and eventually detrimental for what was eternal and liberating in their lives of chastity. They gave up mentalities and bodily indulgences to find God's comforts and hope. For instance, early on, Abba Evagrius struggled with plaguing thoughts of an amorous entanglement he had left behind (and those details are upcoming). He wrote,

> I visited Abba Macarius the Younger, distressed by my thoughts and the passions of the body. I said to him, "My father, tell me a word so I may live." Abba Macarius said to me, "Bind the ship's cable to the mooring anvil and through the grace of our Lord Jesus Christ the ship will pass through the diabolical waves and tumults of this murky sea and the deep darkness of this vain world."
>
> I said to him, "What is the ship? What is the ship's cable? What is the mooring anvil?"

> Abba Macarius said to me, "The ship is your heart. Guard it. The ship's cable is your spirit; bind it to our Lord Jesus Christ, who is the mooring anvil that prevails over all the tumults and diabolical waves that fight against the saints."

So how can you know if your desire is healthy? The elders tell us that a demon of lust or fornication will want ever more and more of you. As it does its work, you will have less and less control over yourself and your focus will be more and more devoted to some self-indulgent activity. God already knows what is hidden. Nevertheless, sometimes we hide the truth from ourselves. Lust enjoys shackling us while telling us that we are free. Little by little, in slipups or in choices that put ourself first, we will find this devil can exert more and more influence. Addiction, compulsion, obsession, and preoccupation are indicators of imprisoning thoughts that harm us through lust. The hermits who chose to live chastely eliminated these consequences from their lives. Though difficult, their lives tell us that temptations can be overcome—and that specific devotional practices can help.

Spiritual Treatments for Lust

The ammas and abbas invite us to be vulnerable before God and live transparently with each other to overcome lust and the other vices. Temptation does not stay at full force during our prayer time—about this they are clear. The elders also tell us to confess and repent if we've fallen short of virtue and right relationship with God or others. They encourage us to have a spiritual friend who can accompany us, at regular intervals. This person is someone with whom we can be honest about each demon that afflicts us, so we don't bear the burden alone. Like an athlete in training needs a coach or training partner to help them stay on track, we should have someone stable, gentle, and kind alongside to benefit our inner life and intimacy with God. They can pray with us in our weaknesses and help us make repentance common—even refreshing. In our context, we can benefit from the guidance of trained spiritual companions.

Be aware that it seems the more effort you put into a chaste or pure life, the more temptation can close in. The elders are clear on this point. So be ready. The more we ask God to purge us of all that is not worthy of our calling, the more we will discover places that need purification and healing through God's love and mercy. If you find more struggles arising as you faithfully confront lust, you're likely pursuing the right course. Buckle in and stay the course.

Moderation is not the method that works with the demon of lust and fornication. Unless this demon is starved to death, it has some power and influence in our lives. Any bit of our attention gives it fuel to grow stronger or be a menace. Over and over, the elders tell us that the battle cannot be a total victory unless the demon has no power—which means it has fled from you. Few elders could attest to true freedom from lust until they had spent *decades* fasting, praying, and living in chastity, humility, and continual devotion to God.

For the rest of us, we should be aware of the sneaky ways we can be influenced and how we are particularly vulnerable to desiring what is inappropriate or harmful. Weeding lust from the garden of our mind is a maintenance project that requires diligence. For our inevitable shortcomings and mistakes along the way, Abba Antony tells us, "To say that God turns away from the sinful is like saying that the sun hides from the blind." I can tell you this, reader: You are loved and forgiven; and when you return to God in repentance, you find relief.

Later we will learn how desert hermit Evagrius found freedom by leaving a dubious situation and practicing a more disciplined kind of life to uproot temptations, including lust. The environments we select and the habits we set determine the particular kinds of temptations we encounter. If lust is the most ferocious demon for you, don't put yourself in situations or continue habits that will make it worse. Don't download the apps, go to the places, have the conversations, or watch the things that make it worse. Maybe we cancel the paid channel, block websites or people, switch where we exercise, or find a hobby that is good for us to replace the one that is not.

It sounds obvious, right? Yes. But sometimes we make things much harder on ourselves with this demon than it ought to be. We forget to be careful. Sometimes we get weary from our diligence, so we start being foolish and careless. And sometimes we may even get to a point where we feel powerless against the problem. What inflames our lust harms our perception and deceives us. Perhaps you already know from experience that the pleasure from pursuing lust or other types of gratification never creates feelings of satiety or lasting satisfaction and peace. That kind of escapade deepens cravings and creates compulsions.

But the desert elders tell us that we have choices. We have agency, and we can flee temptation. Literal fleeing is a righteous option, they say, once things get too hot to handle. Battling with temptation by removing yourself from a situation isn't a path of weakness; sometimes avoiding a situation is the smartest and strongest thing to do. But do take heed: similar temptations can replicate wherever we go, because our issues are also internal. We often contend with these desires repeatedly in other circumstances.

What we give energy and time to will strengthen its hold on us. Consider putting a healthier distraction in your mind that replaces the fantasy—preferably add a spiritual practice. Finally, realize that our thought life is where it all starts and when that aspect is transparent, the light shines on what is rotten and a remedy can come. The abbas and ammas also encourage us to keep at it and stay faithful; living with specific rules and rhythms in our life can help.

Love Is the Whole Story

In the middle of all this talk of impurity, it can be easy to get into a paralyzing shame spiral or just feel, generally, stuck. We realize that we aren't who we want to be, and perhaps we've made mistakes we feel awful about. *Is this a mountain too big to climb?* we may wonder. Or we might think that God likes us less when we fail in this area. Not so.

God's story with us is one of love. That's the whole story. There's no hidden or complex, twisty plotline. After every shortcoming comes a homecoming, if we turn back around. God loves us, but God likes us too. Repentance is not a single choice at a point in time, but a lifestyle we begin to enact—a posture we undertake. As the layers of inner complexity and understanding peel back, what is misaligned can begin to be realigned with God. The Spirit does not reveal to us all that is wrong at once.

We don't have the capacity to see all of that. But with each step of obedience, through each season of our lives, God's ways in us can develop. With more experience, we are rewarded with more insight and grace to hand over to God what can hurt or even destroy us.

When we vanquish the afflicting thoughts, it is not to change God's mind about us. God is Love and God is patient. God hopes that we might not be held captive to anything harmful or degrading because we bear the image of God, our Creator. The story of love cannot be separated from the story of liberty—of our freedom. We can be free from anything that stands in the way of love, glory, and coming homeward to God's embrace. We can enjoy living our best lives and giving back to God ourselves as a living sacrifice no matter what mistakes we've made.

What Mary Aegyptica—the transformed party girl and former seductress of Holy Land pilgrims—found at the Church of the Resurrection in Jerusalem was not God's disgust but God's saving grace, acceptance, and forgiveness. She found new life as God's child, homecoming, and freedom from the shame she felt. And she was forever changed. When we endeavor to battle this demon of lust, we have the love and power of God in us. We can be free.

Reflect and Respond

* What are some impurities of mind or activities you have harbored and would like to be rid of?
* What habits of lust and fornication need healing, forgiveness, and transformation for you?
* What means of support could you use in this process?

Pray

Written by Amma Sarah

O Lord,
You who have measured
The heights and the earth
In the hollow of your hand,
And created the six-wing Seraphim
To cry out to you with an unceasing voice
Holy, Holy, Holy,
Glory to your name.
Deliver me
From the mouth of the evil one, O Master.
Forget my many evil deeds
And through the multitude of your compassions
Grant me daily forgiveness,
For you are blessed unto the ages. Amen.

CHAPTER 3

Ladies of the Realm

Avarice to Generosity

> It is not possessing something that is harmful, but being attached to it.
>
> —Abba Zosimas

In this chapter we meet several wealthy-women-turned-desert-ammas, women who can help us unpack the next afflicting thought: *avarice.* We often use the word *greed* in place of this old-fashioned–sounding word. Originally, greed was associated with overconsumption and overindulging in the sensual aspects of life. Avarice tends to relate to the hoarding of money, wealth, and resources. Though the words *avarice* and *greed* are used synonymously, there are differences.

According to Evagrius, the three temptations of the body are gluttony, lust, and avarice, and to avoid confusing their definitions, let's explain them more now as we encounter them for our purposes. The first one, gluttony, refers to overconsumption of food or other things.

Because gluttony and lust can seem related, sometimes people conflate them. It helps to remember that gluttony is most related to overindulgence. Gluttony most often involves the temptation to overindulge, instead of merely satiate, the bodily appetites of thirst and hunger.

Lust is most connected to inflamed desire. Less frequently, we may think of lust as the intense desire for power, wealth, or other temptations of intense desire. Lust most often refers to a dangerous side of desire that seeks to satisfy itself with inordinate, prohibited, or inappropriate pleasure of a sexual kind.

Greed and avarice both relate to a different kind of disposition: the temptation to keep our abundance to ourselves out of selfish motives. Greed and avarice are desires of the body, categorically speaking, but are different from lust and gluttony because they are less concerned with immediate satisfaction. Greed and avarice are most characterized by accumulation, acute self-interest, and a lack of generosity.

The afflicting thoughts that create temptations of greed and avarice—at least in moments—foil us all. Let's now meet some desert ammas who came from situations in which people are prone to avarice to see what we can learn from their ways and their wisdom. How did they overcome this afflicting thought, how do we encounter it today, and how can we minimize its effect so it has less power in our lives?

Desert Ammas

Most of the ammas whose stories were preserved for posterity came from wealthy backgrounds. Wealthy women are likely remembered more often than impoverished women, because they contributed notable funding and resources to those preserving history. Men were the keepers of history, especially in ancient history. It's likely that these men were beneficiaries of these women's generosity and personally knew of their lives, contributions, and wisdom. Though we do not have many sayings of the desert ammas when compared to the number of sayings and stories from the abbas, nevertheless, with the scraps that remain, we can learn something about them. Their legacy of courage, charity, hospitality, and humility is apparent.

> Let humility become for you the beginning and end of virtues.
>
> —Amma Syncletica

During this period in antiquity there were strict socioeconomic castes, and being a wealthy aristocrat in the Roman Empire meant one had power, resources, civil rights, and legal privileges few had—males or females. In that culture, the home was the domain of the wife, and she could make all the decisions about it. Elite families often owned multiple palatial estates with thousands of acres of working land for farms, flocks, herds, orchards, and fields for grain and vegetables. Add to that the capacity for industry and resources for many fine clothes, luxuries, beauty products, foods, and other possessions. Plus, these families usually owned many hundreds of enslaved people who were forced to work the land, tend their huge homes, and meet every need of their privileged lives. The wealthy had rare access to tutors for a first-rate education, and sometimes enslaved people were trained as scribes to handle reading and writing needs for them. The wealthy also had the ability and desire to travel with a large entourage to help them do it safely and comfortably. Many wealthy Christians spent considerable time visiting the Holy Land and other sites important to them. Some wealthy Christians ended up moving to Egypt, Palestine, or desert areas.

Certain wealthy Christian women, throughout the Roman Empire, functioned more like regal ladies of God's realm rather than royalty of this world. Though most Christians did not go to the desert to live, some offered their homes as a place for church communities to gather. Their level of generosity and faithfulness did not mean they never struggled with avarice, however. Just like we may wonder or worry about the future, they did too. Let's learn of some of them now.

Amma Marcella of Rome

One standout wealthy woman of Aventine Hill in Rome who did not leave for the desert was Amma Marcella (325–410 CE). She was part of the movement that inspired many to live as ascetics by giving up their posh lifestyles and living together as this era of renewed devotion began. After her husband's death, she opened up her opulent home as a communal household for women. She served others, hand and foot, as many of her servants had surely once served her.

Her community of women resided together in a semimonastic manner. They developed their own rule of life by living together faithfully in a specific way with specific expectations. The once high-class women gave up their fancy clothes, fine silks, jewelry, beauty standards, and cushy amenities. Instead, they wore coarse brown garments, and soon Amma Marcella and her followers became known as the Brown Dress Society. They spent time together working, helping the poor and sick, praying, singing, and studying; they maintained a commitment to chastity, fasting, and poverty.

Pause and think for a moment at how loony this would have seemed to all the typical wealthy and entitled people of their day. Friends and associates, outside Christianity, who knew them well would have been outright flabbergasted. Undoubtably, the expectations of the aristocratic class would have put Marcella at odds with everyone in her elite sphere. The pressures and temptations to live as a typical noble person would have been enormous, and her decisions likely brought scorn and difficulty.

Despite likely social pressures of all kinds, Marcella's Rome residence became a fulcrum for plenty of Christian activity and goodwill. Her mother, Albina, and her student and friend, Principia, helped her to establish the community, and later her friend Lea helped her to steward it. These women, and others we will encounter soon, forfeited their special privileges and the temptations to hoard their wealth for their own benefit.

In 382, Jerome, a man now honored as a father of the church, was invited to Rome by Pope Damasus. Marcella hosted Jerome, and he ended up staying at her estate for three years, learning from her in what he called her "domestic church." During that time, he began a close friendship not just with Marcella but with another wealthy widow, Paula (whom we will meet soon). Both women were extremely educated and intelligent. Both assisted Jerome, who was less adept and educated than they were at ancient languages like Hebrew, Greek, and Aramaic. They helped him with his work in translating the Bible into the vernacular of Latin from the Septuagint (Greek Old Testament) and other works, and they funded his work on this and other painstaking projects. The Latin translation of the Bible then proliferated the entire Roman world, and until the 1960s, was used ubiquitously in many millions of church services each day.

Mary, the Sister of Pachomius

Abba Pachomius (292–348), whom we met briefly in the introduction, is often credited with organizing and creating the first communal monasteries in the Egyptian desert. He enlisted the help of his sister Mary. His military training helped him create a functional organization template for success. It's no simple task to have several hundred or even thousands of people living in a tight, interconnected religious community. His format of structure and order made such efforts possible—even grow and flourish. Out in the desert, an enclosure protected their community and buildings. The fortification included specific buildings: a dining area, storehouse, meeting area, buildings for working, a dormitory, and a church where they met twice a day for prayers. The dormitory had a common area for evening gatherings, which included prayers, singing of psalms, and scripture reading. It also contained small cells that held two monastics per room. It's no surprise that monasteries were the birthplace of the first universities—we see this same living format on college campuses today. It began in the desert.

To be admitted as a member in a community organized by Pachomius, one would have to wait outside the gate for a few days and nights, asking to come in. This would show your seriousness, resolve, and willingness to adapt to monastic obedience. Participants were then required to give up their possessions and submit to the community leaders as they centered their life around mutual service. If they were rich, they had to give up any strongholds of avarice and become poor. Desert communities had people dedicated to hospitality for guests and the training of newcomers who wanted to enter the community. New members were helped in their adjustment and mentored for a substantial period of time before they were allowed to participate in communal prayers and activities or reside in a cell.

There were no ordained priests among their numbers, nor did anyone accept a church office position. Though some were leaders, everyone was on equal footing in terms of class. On Sunday, a priest, who had been educated and authorized to preside in liturgical settings, would visit them to celebrate the Eucharist.

Everyone worked with their hands on needed tasks, big and small—even those who came from wealthy backgrounds and who had never served others by hand before. Through making bread, gardening, weaving garments, or cobbling shoes, they could sell items at market to afford other food and supplies and to care for the poor or visiting guests. Though they never ate meat, the residents of Pachomius's communities did not live with the severe austerity of some other desert hermits. They enjoyed vegetables, bread, fish, and fruit once a day.

Pachomius founded nine such communities for male monastics, each with several hundred members, and he set up parallel female communities that functioned the same way. Pachomius asked his sister Mary to superintend the many women seekers as they lived in their own communities. These siblings gave of themselves and their resources to benefit others in a time when the temptation of avarice could have won out. It's reported that some city churches in that period had colluded with the empire to the point that they had abandoned caring for poor widows and orphans. Here we see an example that groups of people, not just individuals, can be guilty of avarice. This may be what incited so many vulnerable women to leave for the desert in search of generous community and equality.

Amma Matrona and Melania the Elder

One of the people who influenced other elites and prompted them to begin humble and generous lives expressed in equality with others was Amma Matrona, who was a contemporary of the Ammas Sarah, Melania the Elder, Theodora, and Syncletica. As sundry wealthy Christian women were widowed, some followed the example of Marcella, Paula, and others. They chose to leave their pampered, socialite lifestyles for the harsh, meager, and largely isolated proto-monastic lifestyle.

What we know of Amma Matrona comes from her profoundly virtuous influence on others—some of them became influential teachers. We will learn more about Amma Matrona and her specific wisdom in later chapters, but for now, we introduce her as one of the inspirations and guides who helped the wealthy Melania the Elder (359–410 CE) leave her wealth and status behind, adjust to the monastic life, and found a monastic community.

Melania the Elder was an extraordinarily well-off woman who came from a Roman senator's family and nobility from Spain. She married and had a son. At age twenty-two, Melania became a widow. Later, she left her son to his life in Rome and thwarted the avarice common to her rank and left for Jerusalem. She was the first to establish a monastery there, at the Mount of Olives, a place that many thousands of Christian pilgrims travelled far to visit. She guided the women who stayed as visitors or the monastics who joined her. Later, a revered abba named Tyrannius Rufinus of Aquileia joined her, and he guided the men.

Before he lived in the desert, Evagrius visited Amma Melania's place in Jerusalem. Melania's wise counsel helped Evagrius emerge from his debilitating spiritual quandary, abandon his illustrious career as the highest-ranked cleric in Constantinople, and take his vows as a monastic. He began this portion of his life under her guidance.

It was Amma Matrona who influenced Amma Melania the Elder. Then Melania the Elder guided Evagrius, who guided many others. Melania the Elder also had a very kind, generous, and devoted granddaughter named after her. Melania the Younger continued her grandmother's work. Amma Melania the Elder's example also inspired Amma Paula to start and fund her own monastic projects in Bethlehem. How beautiful to see a kind of spiritual genealogy—the way one elder influenced another, who influenced another. As these women's ways inspired imitation, their legacies moved from their own realms of dominion outward to be part of the expanding goodness of God's kingdom.

Amma Paula

Amma Paula (347–404 CE) was one of the highest-born elites within the Roman aristocracy in the fourth century. Her family possessed vast holdings in both Greece and Italy. The wealthy, like Paula, were highly educated and powerful, and they often spoke, wrote, and read in a number of languages. Some wrote important letters and commentaries. And as we learned, some even helped with translation work of the Scriptures, as Amma Paula did when she helped Jerome with the creation of the Latin Vulgate—the version of the Bible that had the most profound impact on the medieval church throughout Europe. The cost for translation supplies like vellum and other materials was formidable, and Paula continued as Jerome's financier as his translation work continued for many years.

It all began when Paula left Rome with her daughter Eustochium, Jerome, and likely a large entourage for an extended trip to the desert communities and the Holy Land, where she then settled in and had buildings constructed. This spiritual mother founded two religious communities in Bethlehem. She served as the abbess of the female community, while Jerome took the role of abbot of the male community.

Wealthy women like Paula, and the others we've met, did the culturally unthinkable: They gave up everything to step into lowly positions. When they gave of themselves and their riches to benefit many others in the kingdom of God, they went poor doing it. Through service and generosity, they opposed avarice no matter the personal cost. They also used their financial resources to support other monastic communities in the desert and to take care of the poor, needy, and sick. They created places for safe lodging for the many pilgrims who came to visit the Holy Land sites at the time.

It's hard to imagine the shock that must have reverberated through marbled halls of the elite echelons of the Rome when Paula left everything behind. Some must have thought she had lost her mind, others must have worried for her safety, and some may have wondered if she was being swindled out of her money, by Jerome or whomever else. Whether her neighbors were concerned about her, ridiculing her, or admiring her, one thing was clear: Leaving a luxurious life of plenty for a harsh life of little was a startling change, and few made it. They remain examples of how the rich can pursue a life of righteousness and equality instead of being focused on accumulation, greed, and superiority.

Though this kind of magnanimity was completely unheard of in that era, in my experience, it's awfully rare to see an example of such self-denial now. Such people are atypical because avarice is an insidious and plentiful afflicting thought. It's a demon that the wealthy must battle constantly as they renounce the temptation to sustain their power, access, and wealth. For people of privilege to take on a simple life of self-denial requires divine intervention.

> Those who have endured the labors and dangers of the sea and then amass material riches, even when they have gained much desire to gain yet more and they consider what they have at present as nothing and reach out for what they have not got. We, who have nothing of that which we desire, wish to acquire everything through the fear of God.
>
> —Amma Syncletica

And few would consider making such a sacrifice now. How many of us would choose to sell all we have to benefit the poor and then confine ourselves within a communal structure to serve others hand and foot each day, and live with no comforts—not for a year or two while we are young and healthy, but for the rest of our lives?

Loving Things and Using People

Whether we are wealthy or not, things we use can start to use *us*. All too quickly, the things we love start to deform us into *their* image. Rather than using things—like an apparatus or tool to aid us—we soon begin to esteem and cherish objects or resources in ways that can overshadow our attention and love of other humans. This indoctrinates something worse: Instead of loving people, we can begin to use people, like we use objects or resources. People are more than resources. We can grow selfish and forget.

Thus begins the great avarice reversal: We stop using things and start loving them, and we stop truly loving people and start using them. In this way, a vice—a destructive negative habit—creates a kind of reality distortion field. Treating people poorly starts to get much easier.

It's true even on a small scale. Go to any classic car show, designer outlet shopping store, gun expo, jewelry accessory party, superstore, auction house, motorbike hangout, or bookstore—any place featuring collectibles—and you'll spot how people are bent on possession. Frankly, pick enthusiasts of almost any hobby or fanbase, and see what it entails. You'll find many examples of inordinate attachment and unsettling loyalty to the things at the center of a subculture, over and against empathy toward others. This is the subtle lure of avarice at work.

This type of unhealthy attachment to assets or material things is easy to spot in others. But consider these questions too: What lures me in this way? What resources or objects do I cherish or amass? What would I hate going without or what do I feel I want more of? In what ways have the things I own started to own or influence me?

Amma Syncletica, who used her riches to help others, had a brilliant insight into why Jesus commands almsgiving, or the charitable sharing of one's resources. It's not only for the obvious meaning: helping the poor. Its greater purpose is instilling in us love and mutual concern. This has to penetrate our hearts through actual circumstances. The amma said that in living simply, one can "train the heart for love and compassion" as we look to God for fulfillment. This way, we recognize our source of Love. By giving, we learn to love—in practice—and begin to be moved by love when others are in need.

To those who were very wealthy and chose to live simply, Amma Syncletica said, "You have achieved a small victory with little effort, for you have given away all that is dear to your soul, with one goal in mind; henceforth, direct your gaze to what is greater, namely, to love."

Being Possessed

How interesting that our possessions can become objects that possess us. So easily we begin trusting in our accumulation of things for happiness, security, and provision. Whether it's our assets, savings, or income, this temptation coaxes us to switch our loyalty away from God and center ourselves in our story. Rather than dependence on God, we focus on providing for ourselves.

Have you ever thought, "Maybe buying this or doing this [fill in the blank with an item or an activity] will make me feel better about myself"? Who hasn't? When we succumb to workaholism, we have bought into this mentality. The thinking goes like this, "The more I work, the better off I will be." Often this thinking is labeled as "industrious" by our culture. It is esteemed, even valorized. We hail that person as "a hard worker," and we sense they have integrity. A busy person seems to be an important and reputable person. But the impetus for this hard-driving approach and this behavior comes from the same affliction that tempts a greedy person. It's the same demon, avarice, but it's dressed in respectable attire.

From the standpoint of attachment, we soon lose our freedom. We attach to things and selfish ways of being instead of to a Person outside our circumstances—the Lover of our souls. Once shackled to the idea that our possessions *belong* to us, this initiates a reversal of ownership—as our possessions possess us. They dictate mandates to us, and we serve them. We care for them, clean and preserve them, lock them up for safekeeping, buy insurance policies on them, and of course upgrade them for the next best thing when possible. Sometimes this possessive mentality moves from things to people. We want to upgrade workers, friends, or neighbors. When this happens, we have started to view people as extensions of what we can control or possess in our lives.

Who's really in charge here? With the demon of greed, we do not actually possess any longer—we become possessed. Somewhere along the way, greed assumes control of how we act in the world. When our possessions start to possess us, we are not in control and we are being deceived. It's a common malady.

Wasteful Results

The disordered desire of greed also leads to ugly results such as wastefulness and excessive disregard of resources. This is more common in our day than in the desert era. As a guaranteed by-product, greed creates misappropriation of resources and makes injustice and unfairness not just more likely but part of the bargain. There are countless examples, and I'll mention one specific egregious case of waste.

If you have enough money to buy this book, you likely live within a milieu of abundance and consumerism that creates massive amounts of material refuse. This includes huge burdens of waste from "fast fashion"—cheaply made clothing that we buy inexpensively, wear for a bit, and then toss out. Fast-fashion clothes are purposely fabricated to be temporary because consumers don't want them for long—as a culture, we crave and demand continual novelty in what we wear. For a moment, try to comprehend this statistic: 92 million tons of unused garments end up in landfills each year. This wastefulness includes the practice of illegal dumping from wealthier countries into poorer countries like Chile, Ghana, and Kenya. More vulnerable countries take the brunt of the waste from our collective avarice.

This issue is a relatively new one created in an era when material resources and human labor are valued less than our greed for abundant, fashion-forward clothing at a bargain. Exploitation runs riot. In Chile's Atacma Desert, the colossal clothing pile increases at more than 39,000 tons per year and is so large that it can be seen from space. That's a whopping 78 million pounds, or 31.7 million kilos, of strictly fabric waste accumulating each year! It's difficult to imagine.

This example is only a fraction of the garbage we produce. So many items we think we can't live without are sold in disposable containers and create plastic waste that amounts to 368 metric tons each year. Toxic microplastic now damages our ecosystem—and our bodies. Now up to 90 percent of sea birds contain plastic debris in their bodies.

Avarice always has a sordid underbelly. The results are physically and spiritually toxic.

Prevention Tactics

To move from avarice toward generosity, we need to understand what happens within us as we navigate the territory of greed. When we have a disposition of greed, anxiety and insecurity are central. We may believe that in having something—and then having *more* of it—we will overcome or at least subdue our gnawing sensations of scarcity or feelings of unworthiness. Maybe we will be more accepted by our peers, or garner more status, or be admired in more obvious ways. We may wish to feel more confident or important. In a world powered by avarice, where we live, how we look, the vehicle we drive, the brands we wear, the places we go, how we pamper our pets or children, and the lifestyle we seem to have sends social signals about us. Avarice tempts us to prioritize those over virtue. Peer pressure is not just a middle-school phenomenon. It doesn't go away—it simply shape-shifts. As long as that sort of afflicting thought remains, our selfish ego pilots our lives.

> Just as it is impossible to be at the same moment both a plant and a seed, so it is impossible for us to be surrounded by worldly honor and at the same time to bear heavenly fruit.
>
> —Amma Syncletica

Maybe for one person, greed shows up as collecting fancy watches; maybe for another it's getting the latest crypto coin, phone, or sneakers. For another person it might manifest as hoarding food, medical supplies, or guns and ammo. Or maybe it becomes about something we think is totally benign and widely acceptable, like collecting a sizable portfolio of stocks, bonds, and mutual funds—growing a financial nest egg for later. Plenty of us acquire too many books, clothes, shoes, plants, tools, or kitchen accessories that we don't need, or we give in to impulse buying. Whatever it is, we often think that our treasures will keep us from distress or harm.

But no. Greed offers us a false promise of self-sufficiency. We mustn't forget that no matter the wealth or items we accumulate, we are still at risk. Catastrophe, illness, or diminishment with age will come to all of us. Although our possessions and wealth can connive us into thinking differently, our vulnerability is ever-present. This is a spiritual issue.

In countries of abundance, it can feel risky to live with vulnerability because it is so unfamiliar. But ultimately, it's spiritually healthier to be in a position of trust and interdependence than to be in one of overabundance. What we have will not prevent us from true harm. Jesus tells us that when we try to have it all, we lose our souls (Mark 8:36). None of the things worth having come from the ways of greed, status, or accumulation. The demons of this world, through vice, make false promises that cost us everything dear to us.

Cultivating Interdependence

How much more likely are we to maintain better relationships when we deeply sense that we need others and that others need us? The adage "It's lonely at the top" rings true when it comes to avarice: What autonomy and independence bring us, above all else, are disconnection and spiritual immaturity. Sharing what we have won't keep us at the top, but it will give us our humanity back. This is the lesson that the women from this chapter learned as they renounced possessions and accumulations, gave generously, or moved to desert spaces to live in equality and serve others. They gave up their nest eggs of wealth to build nests for others in the kingdom of God.

Generosity and selflessness can cure the soul sickness of selfishness. Eventually, we will find out the inescapable truth that we can't meaningfully take anything to, or beyond, the grave. Jesus speaks of how foolish the person is who demolishes his grain barns to build new and bigger ones to hold more rather than share with those in need (Luke 22:16). Death is coming for him too; and his selfish life, just like all the extra grain he stored, will come to nothing. Jesus detests stinginess. People who hoard are in essence stealing from others.

Fearing the Future

For the desert dwellers, and for us today, consuming thoughts may afflict us as we begin to reckon with our own avarice. How will we provide for ourselves in old age, or in physical debility, or in times of sickness, calamity, and lack? Furthermore, what if we have no children, as was the case for many of the hermits and monastics of the desert, who eschewed married lives with progeny? Then added concerns can and do arise. "Who will care for me, and how will I afford it?" we think. These are common concerns that cross our minds, and those thoughts are normal, not sinful. Still, we are told to trust God and not accumulate out of fear.

Those of us with less money are not immune from avarice either. Avarice tells us that we can plan ahead and escape pain. Yet avarice cuts off our opportunities to trust and grow faithful. Instead of burning out as we try to meet our own needs, we must see these circumstances as a chance to reflect on and inquire about our deeper issue that relates to trust. Our own efforts of self-provision often usurp our reliance on God's provision. Faithful devotion means we place our concerns about the future all in God's capable hands, come what may. How many of us must confess our lack of faith and renew this intimacy?

Hospitality and generosity were cornerstones of virtue and practice among the desert ammas and abbas. These worked to continually thwart avarice. These desert mothers gave the best of whatever they had to feed and care for the poor and the sick, and to serve guests. When we renew these virtues within us, we make a commitment of a closer walk with God in trust, and we directly benefit others.

Spiritual Practices to Curb Avarice

When we get serious about the ways we are tempted by avarice, we begin to question ideas of ownership. What have we been grasping too tightly? Where is our possessiveness about possessions creating problems? Where are we fixated on accumulation? This is the juggernaut. Three spiritual practices we can employ that keep avarice in check are *generosity*, *simplicity*, and *renunciation*.

In the case of generosity, we practice giving to those in need beyond what feels necessary or comfortable. We can do this with our money but also with our attention, resources, time, and efforts. Ask: In what ways have our interactions become transactional or miserly, and how might we initiate changes? In what ways have we mostly focused on our own best interest rather than living with a generous spirit? We can push back on feelings of discomfort and give more than feels perfectly safe.

With spiritual practices of simplicity, we find ways to rid ourselves of possessions, of values of accumulation, and of status based on what we own or have power over. The habits of "being prepared" drive us to overly accumulate while others suffer in need. We can live more simply than what those around us consider normal. Living more simply frees us from a great many concerns that come with the responsibilities that possessions foist on us.

Renunciation offers a reordered way of being in the world. It might be less familiar than the former two. A life of renunciation enacts our belief that nothing is our own. We keep only a loose attachment to our possessions and have little fear of losing them. Through "mini-deaths," as it were, which sacrifice our comfort in favor of giving to those in need, we can renounce a primary bondage and vice of avarice that can be so imprisoning. As a spiritual practice, renunciation means we can give up some way of being, some thing, or some behavior we've cherished wrongly or too much. It's important to think of this as specifically as possible for your own life. As we live in opposition to greed and avarice, we mortify that which is miserly about us and loosen the grip of these vices on every level possible.

A few ways that subdue avarice and self-sufficiency and that will nurture generosity and interdependence include the following: organizing and living in more intentionally communal ways; canceling or forgiving debts; and realizing our truest wealth lies in our relationships and connections with others and investing there the most.

Belonging and genuine connection are the things money can't buy. The exchanges of camaraderie and goodwill are gifts unavailable to the rich and well-funded, who may grow suspicious of others who seem to desire what they have. Individualism comes up short as it soon becomes interpersonally transactional—it's soulless on a few levels. Money saved and stored can't fill the empty and hollow dimensions that occur when we solve all our own problems. Rather, when interdependency and mutual care are common, more caring relationships and kind exchanges are the norm. Those from hardscrabble communities know this from experience, but in the suburbs and "nicer" neighborhoods, financial autonomy makes such experiences more rare.

It's unlikely that we can recreate the desert communities of old. But we can consider how these people lived together in generosity, hospitality, and simplicity through sharing their resources. It was essential in their rule of life. How can we imitate them? Is it possible to find a few others who agree with a shared set of values that esteem interdependence? Can we invite partnerships as we seek these virtues together? Maybe those ways seem so unfamiliar, not because they aren't feasible, but because they are untried. In what concrete ways can we create aspects in everyday life that mirror those of the desert elders in terms of hospitality or simplicity?

First, we can adjust our lives to be more communally and meaningfully connected with others. This requires starting conversations about mutual aid with others and how we might live differently together. Taking a cue from the abbas and ammas, we can take steps each day to both help and be helped by others. Our lives may change profoundly as we do this.

Ask those who share your values of mutual generosity: What can we share with each other in common? What situations can we help to make more equitable because they are collectively organized? Perhaps your community, church, a few families, or neighbors could explore how to share tools, land, food, vehicles, resources, or certain kinds of access. In what ways can you actively work with others to make interdependence flourish in your family, friendships, neighborhood, or church community?

Reflect and Respond

- What do you treasure or accumulate?
- What are some habits of self-sufficiency that impede your trust and dependence on God?
- What do you admire most about the desert elders so far? Write down a few of those things, and pray your own prayer of renunciation. Ask God to help you give up trusting in your own efforts and to trust God to provide what you need for each day.

Pray

O Lord, I am fully dependent on you.
For each breath and in every gifted moment,
I give you my gratitude.
Help me realize that my self-sufficiency
will cut me off from my own blessing and
from blessing others.
My life is made beautiful through
generosity and interdependence.
Fill me with a grateful heart and a
generous spirit, I ask.
Amen.

Part II

Mind

GO, SIT IN YOUR CELL, AND YOUR CELL WILL TEACH YOU EVERYTHING
ABBA ✦ MOSES

CHAPTER 4

Moses the Strong

Wrath to Meekness

> One who is provoked to wrath by evil thoughts is like a ship on the high seas with a demon for a pilot.
>
> —Abba Evagrius

Things are about to get rowdy. The abba we learn about now once had a violent, crime-filled life.

One of the most inspiring desert stories of transformation is that of beloved Moses the Strong (330–405 CE). He was known to his contemporaries as Abba Moses, among other names, and he helps us deal with the devil of wrath. Abba Moses testified that he warred mightily for many years to overcome all the afflicting thoughts. His example could help us with any of them, although he would have been much too humble to say so.

His story begins in Ethiopia, his birthplace—years before the apostle Paul started missionary journeys and church planting, this area was changed by the gospel due to the royal eunuch of Queen Candance who encountered the apostle Phillip

(Acts 8:26). By the time Moses was born, Christianity was practiced and accepted in the areas of Ethiopia and Nubia. King Ezana (320s–360 CE) made Christianity the official religion of the powerful Kingdom of Aksum in 330 CE—making it one of the first countries to do so.

Moses's story reminds us that the continent of Africa is a vibrant part of God's kingdom and has brought us the gospel from the very beginning and remains unbroken to this day. To miss this point is to miss much about the history and endurance of the Christian faith. As certain as the earliest instances of Christianity are rooted in Africa is the fact that damaging prejudice and racism taints much of how Western narrators have described Africa's people. Certain accounts about Abba Moses contain distinctly racist elements. Please refer to the Author's Note at the end of this book for my comments on this.

Moses's life was marked by hardship, beginning when he was kidnapped as a child from his family in Ethiopia. He was exploited in forced labor by a high-ranking government official in the thriving Roman metropolis of Alexandria, Egypt. This type of appalling childhood was not uncommon in the ancient world, and surely these early traumas in Moses's life wounded him deeply and fed his temptations of wrath and vengeance to come.

In many ways, Moses was a larger-than-life personality, but he grew to be physically big and strong, too. In our context, the world of professional wrestling would welcome someone of his imposing size and strength. The older he got, the more intimidating and vengeful he became. He could put a smack down on anyone.

As a youth, Moses also began to take things that weren't his. It's ironic, of course, that kidnappers keen on stealing children for free labor get irrationally upset when they are stolen from. Nevertheless, rather than bring formal charges against Moses, who would probably have faced death for his infractions, his enslaver dismissed him—though accounts of what happened differ. Some say he ran away from his situation, and some say he killed someone beforehand. But whatever happened, Moses set off and roamed the area, looking for job opportunities that called for brawn.

According to his own accounts, Moses soon fell in with a horde of violent pillagers numbering over seventy people. They accomplished crime spree after crime spree. Just pause for a moment and imagine it: Raucous raiders, by the dozens, moving from one little town to the next, smashing stuff, taking things, throwing people around, and doing whatever they wanted. What a brutal lifestyle.

The key members of this posse soon recognized Moses's cleverness, fearlessness, and physical prowess—and seeing that skill set, they put him in charge. With his quick ascension to boss status, he now directed the mob of bandits and started living the ultimate thug life. Along with the rest of them, Moses was sinning like a professional in all kinds of ways: attacking, murdering, thieving, injuring, plundering, drinking heavily, fornicating, and inciting mayhem galore. Ranchers, travelers, and whole towns feared this band. As Moses and his pillaging delinquents were terrorizing the area and creating chaos far and wide, certain officials began trying to track him down.

As he was on the run from authorities, Moses hid with the isolated monastic community in Scete led by Abba Isidore. During his visit, Moses watched the brothers closely over a period of days. Their peace and contentment surprised him, and their kindness amazed him. No one seemed to want to kill, steal, or destroy. What would that kind of life be like, he wondered? And just like that, Moses decided to give up his hooligan ways.

But it's not so easy to have a life makeover when you're a fiery Shaq-sized man with bad habits who's fresh out of work as the boss of a violent cadre of bandits. These are not snap changes that come easily, and as you might guess, his infamous reputation had preceded him, even in the far-flung desert city of Scete. The community wasn't just afraid of him; they had serious doubts that he truly wanted or could make a career change and turn his life around. Would this hot-tempered thief and murderer really live peacefully among them for the long term, they wondered?

Lovingly, Abba Isidore extended welcome to Moses and began to teach him. After a short time, Moses learned the gospel. He repented of and confessed his sins. Then he was baptized into Christianity as a follower of Jesus by the big-hearted Abba Macarius the Great, whom we will learn about soon.

But would such repentance stick? The community was still wary of him and kept their distance a bit, but Abba Isidore had a compassionate heart for Moses and assisted him with guidance and grace. Though glad about Moses's signs of repentance from a degenerate life, Abba Isidore had concerns that Moses was wildly underestimating how difficult full-time monastic life would be. Desert asceticism is arduous and full of missteps for any person, and given how undisciplined and indulgent Moses had been, such a decision obviously meant many painful lessons and failures were upcoming. Would the effort be fruitful, or was failure assured?

After Moses's conversion experience, Abba Isidore guided him for a time with gentle compassion, but before long Abba Isidore tried to send Moses on his way. He hoped Moses could begin a new but ordinary life of righteousness: with church support in a town without all the strict requirements of their community. Abba Isidore tried to send him on his way a few times, but Moses didn't want to start over somewhere else. Contrite and determined, Moses wept and wept and wouldn't leave. His mind was made up: He wanted to adjust to desert life and be a brother to the ascetics there. After seeing his deep conviction and persistence, the brothers of the community and the other leaders in Scete accepted him not as a guest passing through but as one of their own.

As anyone would predict, monastic transformation became grueling. Moses spent decades severely grappling with temptations. He recounted that the memories of his unlawful acts, his wanton brutality, and ongoing temptations drove him nearly mad. As he battled nonstop with afflicting thoughts, he regularly sought the counsel of his spiritual father, Abba Isidore, who later remarked on Moses's hard-won and drastic spiritual change in the ensuing decades. Instead of sleeping, Moses began to spend nights in prayer and traveling far off to the well. In kind and humble service to the brothers, he refilled water containers for the monks as they slept.

Early on during his time in Scete, Moses apprehended and tied up four would-be assailants who came to raid the monastic community. The four men were stunned because they recognized Moses as their former crime boss. He slung all four of them over his back and carried them to the abbot in charge to determine next steps. Surely, they were going to meet a grisly demise, they thought.

But the abbot told Moses to free the four bandits. Moses obeyed, and the four men were stupefied. What had happened to the violent and vengeful criminal they had known? Why wasn't he going to hurt or punish them? Would he simply set them free?

This was no longer the same kind of man. Moses's transformation created such astonishment and curiosity in them that it wasn't long before they, too, joined the community and turned their lives around, just as he had done. In the end, Moses the merciless outlaw became a gracious pacifist. A gentle giant. All his wrath eased into meekness.

One account that attests to Abba Moses's transformation, humility, and compassion occurs after he was made the head abba of his own community in his old age. Once there was gathering called to determine the course of action for a member who had committed an infraction. As the founding father of this community, Abba Moses was expected to be there and invited to preside.

But Moses refused to attend. As the rest of the community gathered, the priest sent someone to tell him, "Come, for everyone is waiting for you." Abba Moses found a ruptured container, filled it with water, and took it with him to the gathering. When the monks noticed water dripping out, they asked what he was doing. Abba Moses said, "My sins run out behind me, and I do not see them, and today I am coming to judge the errors of another."

Boom. What a mic drop! They understood the lesson, dispersed, and forgave their brother.

From violent to peaceful, from egotistical to humble, from short-tempered to long-suffering, from foolish to wise: Abba Moses's transformation influenced many hundreds of lives directly and countless others indirectly. Hundreds of monastics flourished under his guidance. The stories of his legendary goodness, wisdom, and humility spread, and many visitors came seeking his counsel. Dignitaries and students alike sought to sit at his feet and learn from him. So dramatic was his story of transformation that a number of criminals from his former crime cohort also repented and joined the monastic community to live new lives of peace. Their devotion turned to God instead of their selfish pursuits.

After a long life that was a testament to devotion, discipline, and transformation into Christlikeness, Moses foresaw an impending attack on the community that would devastate the community and lead to his own death. He warned the monastics to flee and relocate, but he would not go with them. The brothers pleaded over and over again for him to accompany them as they evacuated their home, but he told them that an appropriate and fitting death was coming to him. Echoing the sentiment and words of Jesus, he told them that he had "lived by the sword" and now he should also "die by the sword."

Almost everyone in the community fled to safety, but a handful stayed at Abba Moses's side. Just one monk escaped with his life after the raid, and he became a witness to Moses's peace-saturated demise. This dear and tender Abba Moses was known as immensely humble and he finished his life empty of violence, wrath, and selfishness.

Abba Moses willingly chose to be killed without fighting back at all. He is now known in the Eastern Orthodox, Oriental Orthodox, and Catholic churches as the patron saint of nonviolence and is celebrated by millions on his feast day, every August 28.

Anger and Wrath

Abba Moses gives us courage and wisdom to tackle the difficult issues of anger and wrath with which so many of us struggle. Maybe we have seen how these vices can incinerate relationships and create a multitude of harms. Perhaps we have wrestled with these afflicting thoughts ourselves, or watched loved ones succumb to it. Whether we brashly express our anger or keep it shoved down, this emotion is hazardous.

First, let's notice how anger and wrath, for our purposes, are two different issues. You have likely seen the words *anger* and *wrath* used interchangeably, but here I use each of them distinctively. Simply put, anger is less costly than wrath. Anger is a reaction of emotion. Wrath is stored.

Recent neuroscientific discoveries find something surprising about all emotions, including anger. Emotions are not what happens in *response* to a situation. Instead, our brain *creates* emotions. Based on our past experiences and the current stimuli our bodies sense, our brain *predicts* our emotions as our body senses our situation. Our brain tries to match the interpretation of the present situation we are sensing, not matched to reality, but to what it already knows.

In other words, our emotions don't sit at a dashboard in our brain and push certain buttons so we feel anger, sadness, disgust, or joy based on how things are, as some animated movies might have us conceptualize (as adorable as those depictions are). We don't perceive reality as it truly is and then experience emotions accordingly in an accurate manner. Rather, we perceive reality as previous experiences have shaped and conditioned us to understand it. Our brain excels at finding patterns and making meaning of what we perceive; then it nearly instantly produces emotions, thoughts, and feelings that pair to these *predictions*.

This is why people who have been traumatized will get highjacked by big emotions. It's why even kin or close friends can have radically different responses to the same occurrence. Or why combat veterans or those who've been abused will be triggered by what may seem to others like something ordinary.

Say that two people witness a car accident. One person may feel sympathy and the other anger. Or say a colleague receives an accolade; one coworker may feel envy and another might feel gladness. People have a variety of emotional reactions to the same incident because their brains are predicting differently based on past experiences.

Moses needed to heal from his past hurts and his violent past so he could attain peace and feel safe. Until then, his brain would make rash or fear-based predictions. His desert spiritual practices helped.

Since our brains have plasticity, that means they respond as we retrain them through attention, new practices, and habits. Our feelings and responses, just after our initial misguided emotions, can be regenerated to be more accurate, over time, as we finally feel safe, healed, loved. With practice, and through reflection, time, and effort, we can regulate ourselves better—even with our most fiery emotions. It happens when we begin to perceive and predict differently. We let love in to change us.

In the community at Scete, this is how Abba Moses turned from wrathful to meek. Remember, he had been kidnapped from his family and forced into labor as a young child. He would have felt frightened, angry, and downright powerless. These events, and likely many other harms, surely affected him. As Moses got big enough to inflict injury and even death on others, he did. But that was not the end to his story. He became a hero of the faith.

Just like Moses and all the desert elders, we can, with God's help, heal from the experiences that have created emotional wounds within us. Instead of responding with angry knee-jerk reactions, like the beloved Moses the Strong once did and many of us do, we can find freedom and learn to respond differently.

Our brains' poor speculations can be changed with reflection and self-knowledge plus spiritual practices, which cultivate healing and lead to awareness and freedom.

Without finding any healing or doing any training, we tend to experience reactive emotional states and spiritual immaturity. The desert dwellers practiced this sort of effort and training within their rule of life. We, too, can eventually develop into more emotionally balanced people who seldom have outbursts of rage or wrath.

Anger Is Not a Sin

Many of us have overly attached to an emotion like anger. We might describe ourselves, or someone else, as "an angry person" rather than a person who experiences anger. Our language divulges our misperception. Many of us feel so proximal to anger that we feel fused to its character. We may begin to find an identity within it. Other emotions, and even vices, can work that way for us also.

It can be freeing to realize we are not our thoughts and emotions. They are things we experience. They are separate from us, and issues we can begin to understand more fully, and then curtail. It was Evagrius who helped me notice how emotions, feelings, and temptations move into and out of our inner landscape, like weather systems move through literal mountain and valley landscapes. Emotions and feelings come and go. It is imperative to note the separation, because in understanding ourselves as distinct from what we feel, we grow more empowered to make adjustments.

Pay close attention to this: Our initial anger is an emotion, not a sin. This may be a new concept to many of us who were raised to believe that anger is a sin. Categorically, initial anger fits in the same box as pain. I hope no one would claim that crying out in pain when we slice open our finger is a sin. Now, if we cut ourselves . . . and then punch someone in the throat, that's different. We've sinned in anger at that point.

When we are habituated as reactive people, we are less inclined to notice the space *between* an initial reaction and a secondary response. We are less able to comprehend how they are in fact two separate things. Any naturally occurring human emotion is not sinful as it first arises. After our original emotional response, we make a choice about what to do. For some of us, there comes a nearly instantaneous response to emotion, and we may misunderstand the emotion and the response as happening at the same time. These responses might be either harmful or wise. Those who haven't separated the *sense* of emotion from the *expression* of the emotion are prone to ongoing "anger issues." But with healing, growth, and training, pure reacting eases into something more thoughtful soon after: responding wisely.

The desert elders give us many cautions about untrained anger—saying we must learn to rein in this short-lived emotion like we would a powerful, toothy beast. They remind us that our best example is Jesus, who is also recorded as having moments of short-lived anger. Never does Jesus stay angry or nurse a grudge. In fact, he tells us to show love to even our enemies. He tells us that he has not come to act like a wrathful judge (John 12:47). Of all people who could judge, he would be the appropriate one for the job. Instead, he chooses forgiveness. "Father, forgive them for they don't know what they are doing," he says while being executed like a criminal though he had not committed any capital offense (Luke 23:34). He says this not in anger but with compassion.

Stored Anger Spoils

Anger, when it is stuffed down, can turn into hopelessness, self-despising, and despair. Never forget that once anger is stored, its shelf life is terrible. It soon rots into a reeking social and spiritual poison: wrath. Now it possesses destructive qualities. Rage is an example of unexamined stores of anger that become explosive and create destruction. Bitterness, resentment, envy, spite, indignation, cynicism, and irascibility are all by-products of stored anger, too. Rage breaks the dam that has been holding back the coming wreckage of wrath. It is wrath that may cause us to misperceive and thereby create damage that cannot be undone. There is no counting the many acts of violence or destructive words that have come through the vice of wrath: the stored anger that has bested humankind.

> Bear your own faults and not to pay attention to anyone else wondering whether they are good or bad. Do no harm to anyone, do not think anything bad in your heart towards anyone, do not scorn the person who does evil, do not put confidence in the person who does wrong to their neighbor, do not rejoice with a person who injures his neighbor. . . . Do not rail against anyone, but rather say, "God knows each one."
>
> —Abba Moses

Since anger is the emotion that spoils us, the apostle Paul cautions us not to "let the sun go down on your anger" (Ephesians 4:26). Nothing good will happen once anger hardens into a grudge or cements into hurt feelings. Since anger metastasizes into wrath, we must forgive each other, make amends, solve problems together, or negotiate better circumstances before anger rots in us and damages our lives. New mornings have new mercies.

Dragon's Wine or Angel's Bread?

Abba Evagrius says the most damaging of the afflicting thoughts is wrath. "A boiling of irascibility" is how the abba describes it. *Irascible* is a little-used word now, but it connotes a quick-tempered, irritable, and easily annoyed way of being. A person with a short fuse is irascible, ready to lash out or set to explode—a person actively storing anger. There is a disposition of crankiness and inhospitality—a combination that is the opposite of grace or meekness. No one seeks out or enjoys the company of an irascible person. Interactions are fraught and unpleasant.

Abba Evagrius called wrath "dragon's wine." This creates interesting imagery—a menacing combo of fire, intoxication, and beastly monstrosity. A chronically angry person takes things personally, is quickly offended, and is chronically fearful too. No one delights in a drunk fire-breathing dragon. Some people filled with dragon's wine exploit their wrathful ways so that others fear them and concede. They think wrath makes people respect them, but they become despised and resisted. Some aren't aware that their explosions have the effect they do.

So what can be done? The solution to the dragon's wine of wrath is what Abba Evagrius calls "angel's bread." We might think peace, calmness, or passivity would be the opposite of wrath. But no. According to many of the desert elders, the virtue that is the opposite of wrath is meekness. Meekness is not some merger of mildness and weakness. It is the hearty provision of angels: a courageous and stable humility of heart.

Evagrius assures us that meekness is a prerequisite for prayer. Without it, we don't have the disposition to pray with a pure heart. God calls us to meekness, and Jesus's life was saturated with it. Just like food keeps us healthy, the gift of meekness is spiritual food that nurtures us in crucial ways. Jesus said he was the Bread of Life—gentle and humble in heart. In desert spirituality, we partake in the spiritual food of meek Jesus himself that we may eat the food of eternal life and become what we eat (John 6:53).

What About Holy Anger?

So is there a place for expressing anger? Absolutely—anger is an appropriate response to injustice. The crux of the issue is *how* we express such anger. This makes all the difference. Instead of making our anger a flamethrower we expel onto others, we offer our anger up, just as it is, to Someone who can really handle it: God. This is how anger becomes holy.

If we can be honest about how we feel without hurting others or creating more harm, through such things as prayer and other creative expressions, then our anger helps us and others without catching everything ablaze. Socially and spiritually, we have much to gain this way. It's the easy and undisciplined thing to have an angry outburst. But to resolve problems in other ways? That takes true strength.

Communally, anger works the same way. As a community, we may start from a place of anger at some injustice, problem, or hurt. Then we must act wisely and work together to express what is happening for a long-term benefit, not just a shortsighted release or retaliation. The creative arts can help us process the emotion of anger expressively or bodily better than anything. With a holy imagination, we can find opportunities to convey what's wrong through oration, peaceful activism, nonviolent protest, or art forms like music, dance, drama, visual media, or poetry. Such anger will serve us well as a catalyst, but only if it's diffused into what can be generative and shouldered together. If the energy can be directed at confronting and dismantling evil instead of seeking vengeance or exacting retribution, then the demon of wrath won't manipulate us. Justice does not mean just evening the score; it's enacting mercy when the debt is too large and enforcing means of reparations so restoration becomes possible. In our anger, rage, or wrath, we usually fail to see this.

Anger and Leadership

Sometimes leaders, even in religious settings, exist in a culture where it's permitted to express anger in harmful ways—and sometimes followers are not permitted to express any anger. In many places, like sporting events, boardrooms, or the public square, men are lauded as "passionate" when they express wrath in public, while women can incur various harms or social penalties for expressing it.

So what role should anger play in leadership? A wise spiritual mother can speak to this. Amma Theodora cautioned that a leader must have specific qualities, including a right relationship with anger. "A teacher ought to be a stranger to the desire for domination, vainglory, and pride," she writes. "One should not be able to fool [them] by flattery, nor blind [them] by gifts, nor conquer [them] by the stomach, nor dominate [them] by anger; but [they] should be patient, gentle and humble as far as possible; [they] must be tested and without partisanship, full of concern, and a lover of souls. . . . Neither asceticism, nor vigils, nor any kind of suffering are able to save, only true humility can do that."

When these qualities that Amma Theodora mentions are in short supply in leaders and systems, situations of abuse can harm millions. What kind of world would we have if our spiritual leaders had followed Amma Theodora's advice from the start?

Desert wisdom is clear: Meekness can defeat the poisonous effects of anger and make a person worthy of being followed. In our times, leaders often exert influence by peacocking and platforming and posturing to boost their cult of personality. They may think dominance rather than humility shows they are worthy to lead. But they couldn't be more wrong.

It's time to revive desert spirituality for our times and make meekness our main aspiration again—not just for leaders, but for all of us. Meekness is an attribute only others can ascribe to us. As soon as we notice our own prowess when it comes to humility, it vanishes. Our meekness is known in our deference to others and willingness to show strength in countercultural ways.

The kind of person Amma Theodora advises us to choose as a leader—or to make sure we become as a leader—is rare. Such leaders don't manipulate others, minimize abuses of power, shirk responsibility, or step on people to get ahead. They won't make their members or staff sign nondisclosure agreements to protect themselves and hide their bad behavior. The godly leader will ditch their ego for God's ways and will be gracious and loving to those who follow them. Let us be sure to regularly reevaluate our relationship with anger and wrath, and the other qualities that may trip us up, especially if we have leadership roles.

What Makes Anger Righteous?

Righteous anger relates directly to creating and maintaining right relationships. Have you ever witnessed a chronically angry person holding up the example of Jesus angrily driving out the temple money changers as a free pass to lash out in a confrontation or stew on rage? This is a case of wildly missing the point.

What we notice when we look at the passage (Matthew 21:12) is that Jesus wasn't having an outburst because his rights were denied or his ego was offended. He was angry *in the defense of and on behalf of others* who were powerless to change their situation. Why? In this case, because profiteers had converted the temple court of the Gentiles area, which was a place for prayer, into a marketplace known for its corruption. They had businesses and a currency exchange system that was cheating poor people out of what little money they had. How outrageous it was to pervert the house of God this way. But who could stand up to these money-grubbers who were in cahoots with the Temple authorities?

With a righteous zeal for those crushed by the system of injustice and avarice, Jesus stepped in, confronted the racketeers, and disrupted their dealings. The religious power elites didn't appreciate it, though. The incident led to temple authorities plotting his arrest soon after.

Notice the difference. Here was righteous anger with *someone else's benefit in mind.* Our anger is a just and righteous anger when we respond to situations where evil is called good and when wrongs have been overlooked. It is the kind of situation that looks not for revenge but to make things right again. It centers fairness and grace to those dispossessed of resources, privilege, and power.

Let us never keep anger stored inside until it becomes distorted and warps into resentment and rage that will not stop until it enacts a form of punishment. Punishment is how too many people misconceive justice, but this is foolish and shortsighted misunderstanding. Anger and wisdom don't keep company with each other. The wisest person has overcome the weakness of unmastered anger. For that person, initial anger is used toward positive change and stays short-lived. Wrathful retribution or immature, ego-driven reprisals are at odds with holy anger.

The Cussing Scriptures

The man who brought the desert teachings and monastic ways of living westward to Europe, John Cassian, noted wisely that all forms of anger "blind us in prayer." He speaks here of being hindered from praying effectively. So perhaps the best way to contend with anger is to give it to God and allow it to diminish. Otherwise, our prayers will not have much effect to help us. The abbas advising Moses the Strong guided him this way also.

Let's pause for a few moments and ask ourselves: What would a prayer that offers our anger to God sound like?

It might sound a little like one of the psalms. A prayer that lifts our anger to God requires that we be honest about our anger. The imprecatory psalms, also called "the cursing psalms," make up a sizable portion of the psalms in the Bible. I'm relieved such furious song prayers are included in the canon of Scriptures. One of them goes: "Let death stalk my enemies; let the grave swallow them alive, for evil makes its home within them" (Psalm 55:15). We are invited, also, to tell God our honest feelings. Such expressions of anger, ferocious words and all, make way within us for God to help us handle these hardest and most wearying trials. By this, we can offer up our fears and rage and live in a manner of ongoing trust with the Divine. Through the cussing psalms, we don't have to have it all figured out or wage an attack on our enemies. We can leave anger behind. We can avoid trying to remedy our problems with wrath. Regardless of how we feel, we are responsible for how we handle our anger. For it to be righteous, anger cannot be harmful.

Being honest about our anger often reveals our deeper sadness or grief. For that we need lament. But *communal* lament is what we need to live sustainably in healthy ways. Psalms of lament are another category of psalm, and all the psalms of lament in the Bible were poetry written to be sung by a community. The wails and the tears of suffering were not to be kept private, but to be witnessed, heard, and acknowledged. All the difficult emotions were to be given space and voice. This process of moving through grief and bereavement, which is losing someone close to us, should be shouldered together. We as individuals should never have to endure such times alone.

In places like the contemporary United States, we often hurry past tragedy and keep our pain locked in and to ourselves. Horrendous violence surrounds us in the most monstrous ways each day, and we keep moving along isolated from help and without grieving. We don't give ourselves any time to metabolize what's happened so we can acclimate to life again after pain recedes. The fiery pain is only buried just below the surface. This creates destructive emotional wounds and cognitive dissonance that harm us in the long term and often perpetuate more harm, chaos, and violence. It seems the ancients knew how to acknowledge anger, grief, and suffering and work through pain *collectively* better than we do now. They didn't have the technology to kill and harm at the rates we do, and yet they eclipse us in slowing down to heal and knowing how crucial the grieving process is to mitigate more harm.

Imperturbability is what meekness looks like in action. That's worth reading again. The desert elders teach that imperturbability is a prerequisite for effective prayer. The wisest elders inhabited the world as people who had a non-anxious presence about them. They were a guiding light for their students and those who visited. They were not tossed on the waves of anger or oceans of anxiety, because they had been molded into brave and meek students of Jesus—the Savior who was famous for napping on stormy seas.

Abba Moses imparted his students with many pieces of wisdom, and so it seems fitting to end this chapter with some of his words. May they inspire us on how to live well with others and how to avoid storing negative emotions, including anger. Abba Moses says, "Do not agree with a person who slanders, do not rejoice at their slander and do not hate a person who slanders their neighbor." He continues by clarifying, "This is what it means not to judge. Do not have hostile feelings towards anyone and do not let dislike dominate your heart; do not hate a person who slanders his neighbor. This is what peace is: Encourage yourself with this thought, 'Affliction lasts but a short time, while peace is forever, by the grace of God the Word.'"

Reflect and Respond

- What about Abba Moses's story stands out to you?
- What might be the pain, sadness, or fear that produces anger and wrath for you?

* What patterns do you notice in your hurts, disappointments, and frustrations that produce anger or wrath?
* What sorts of things can make you take offense, perhaps too easily? How might those things be connected to your sense of ego?

Pray

Show me, oh Lord, if I grieve your Spirit with my anger and my wrath
Confront me with my unholiness that I may confess it to you fully
I sacrifice, to you, my need to be right, that creates offense within me
I repent of the incendiary fires I ignite that damage me and those you love
Give me the heart of Abba Moses, whose heart was made tender by you
Comfort me with your presence
Amen.

CHAPTER 5

Wee Abba John

Acedia to Faithfulness

> Whether or not all these thoughts trouble the soul is not within our power; but it is for us to decide if they are to linger within us or not and whether or not they stir up [sinful desires].
>
> —Abba Evagrius

As you have learned by now, the real-life cast of characters in the desert era includes all sorts of people. The much beloved Abba John (339–407 CE) was a wise and memorable man affected by dwarfism. Though he was small, his goodness and piety grew large, and he attracted many disciples. He was born of poor parents in Thebes, Egypt, and left for the desert way of living at just eighteen years old. In the Scete community, he labored against his demons under the direction of Abba Pambo, who had once been a disciple of Antony the Great, Father of Monks; Pambo was financially supported by the gracious Melania the

Elder. One of the elders lovingly said of John, "Who is this John, who by his humility has all Scete hanging from his little finger?"

Abba John wove baskets that he sold to meet his basic needs. Like most monastics, he prayed while he worked. While in deep prayer, he would sometimes lose track of how big his basket was getting. He spent so much time in ongoing prayer while he wove baskets that sometimes his weavings would fill his entire living space. Picture that! A visitor to his cell would encounter an enormous basket with a small hermit, caught in the rapture of praying while weaving inside it.

Abba John was known for his fervent commitment to prayer in solitude—so much so that, for more seclusion, he once decided to leave the confines of his cell to avoid distractions and visitors and burrow into a space that he dug out of the ground himself. I can't help picturing him tunneling furiously into the ground like a badger to get some peace.

According to the stories, his spiritual father once gave his student John an absurd and epic task. Abba Pambo plunged a dry stick into the sand and told young John to water it every day, twice, until it bore fruit. As the story goes, John had to walk for twelve miles to get water for this assignment. Sometimes he had to leave in the evening and return the following morning to do it.

Finally, at the end of three years, the little twig sprang to life. The abba exalted John's faithfulness among the community and called the fruit that came from that watered stick "the fruit of obedience." John was ordained a priest and years later, just prior to the final raid that destroyed the community, he left for Suez and the Mountain of Anthony.

"I think it best that a person should have a little bit of all the virtues," Abba John taught. "Therefore, get up early every day and acquire the beginning of every virtue and every commandment of God. Use great patience, with fear and long-suffering, in the love of God, with all the fervor of your soul and body."

Abba John seemed especially attuned to his vulnerabilities, and he advised his students regarding faithfulness by teaching them, "Persevere in keeping vigil, in hunger and thirst, in cold and nakedness, and in sufferings." This is a form of prayer we can also call *holy waiting*.

> I think it best that a person should have a little bit of all the virtues.
>
> —Abba John the Small

Abba John kept his teachings practical and simple. They center on steadfast faithfulness and humility toward God and others. Like all the monastics, Abba John struggled with afflicting thoughts as he matured spiritually. In this chapter, we'll look at the temptation of acedia (pronounced: ah-*seed*-dee-ah) that we all face. Though we don't know whether acedia was among his worst struggles, we do know that early on he was tested with the stick-watering assignment, which likely created afflicting thoughts of acedia during the process. Perhaps that's why Abba Pambo gave him such a task in the first place. We remember not that he faltered but that he stayed diligent.

Acedia was a common temptation for the desert dwellers, and it remains a prevalent affliction of our times. Abba Evagrius knew how important it was to warn novice monastics and students about acedia. Now we will take some time to explain it.

In the list we call the seven deadly sins, sloth replaced acedia. Sloth means *a reluctance to make an effort or work* as it relates to enacting God's priorities, like helping the needy or being devoted. Acedia is the tempting feeling that happens prior to choosing to be slothful. Acedia literally means "lack of care." For desert-dwellers, acedia related to the temptation to stop caring about what they were there for and leave for somewhere else. Though not a familiar word for many of us now, acedia, generally speaking, exerts command in our inner world. It also has influence on our society more generally. Most perniciously, it works against our relationships and impedes our spiritual advancement.

Unpacking Acedia

We can be plagued by the afflicting thought of acedia when we first sense a persistent feeling of malaise or meaninglessness that clouds our perspective. In these times, we don't exactly know what's wrong with us when it comes to acedia. But sometimes when life does not feel like a gift or a joy, acedia will tempt us into deeper feelings that everything we are working toward is now tedious and consequently too difficult to continue. We also may feel separated from our purpose or communion with God.

Amma Syncletica shared wisdom on the kind of acedia that shows up in the form of restlessness. When we are tempted to think we'd be happy if we just lived somewhere else, had a different job, we had married someone else, or had other opportunities, then acedia might be afflicting us. To the neophyte monastics, Amma Syncletica said, "If you find yourself in a monastery do not go to another place, for that will harm you a great deal. Just as the bird who abandons the eggs that she sits on prevents them from hatching, so the monk or the nun grows cold and their faith dies when they go from one place to another." Amma Syncletica witnessed the enticement to flit from one place to the next, or be lured from one exploration to the next one, even in religious pursuits. The next adventure is often a tempting substitute for spiritual growth. When we begin deeper internal work, it always becomes uncomfortable. Novel and absorbing situations eventually become mundane. So it's common to give in to our restless temptations of acedia. The elders taught that restlessness could be overcome by faithfulness.

Acedia can also be described as listless soul-weariness or crippling apathy. Someone in the throes of acedia might use such phrases as "being burned out," "feeling restless," or "having the blahs," and may be quite unaware that they are struggling with acedia. It's common for many of us to get stuck with this afflicting thought after making a tough but important life decision. Once we hit a rough patch in a challenging pursuit like starting a new project, learning a skill, pursuing further education, joining the military, getting married, or beginning anything lengthy and difficult, we may bump up against such temptation. The temptation is normal, but knowing how acedia can ensnare us can help us avoid a frustrating entanglement with it.

Abba Evagrius called this temptation the most oppressive devil. For his students, he termed it something very specific: "the noonday demon." He witnessed how attacks of acedia often visited monastics in the hottest and most uneventful stretches of the day. At specific hours, between about 10 a.m. and 2 p.m., acedia tempted desert seekers the most, he noticed. It lured them to leave their cells and stop their prayers. Sometimes it led them to consider abandoning their community, their rule of life, and their vows—to leave it all for a new situation or more pleasurable adventures.

This exact variety of uncomfortable boredom the desert monastics experienced is quite rare in our day, because we usually have so many things to entertain and distract us the instant we feel bored, or even mildly unamused. But underlying our persistent scrolling on our phones or busy schedules is the same strange and gnawing affliction and the accompanying temptation to break free or find a solution. Something doesn't seem right, and while we may not know what it is, we feel anxious about it. We've all been there.

In her book *Acedia and Me*, writer Kathleen Norris notes that acedia also presents itself in our context as "fashionable cultural melancholy." It's in vogue to be chronically dissatisfied. Acedia stays on as a persistent discontent with all that is not new, novel, or propelling our fascination. Norris goes on to say, "Acedia has come so far with us that it easily attached to our hectic and overburdened schedules. We appear to be anything but slothful, yet that is exactly what we are, as we do more and care less, and feel pressured to do still more." How's that for tricky?

Let's go deeper still. Hallmarks of acedia can include a lack of spiritual joy and a persistent sense of unease. We may stay on agitated alert, waiting for the better option to pop up or for some excitement in some other area to divert us. Therefore we stay noncommittal. We fail to dig deeply and invest in where we actually are. A slump of ennui gives us a trapped feeling, and the doldrums of apathy hinder us on matters that we would otherwise consider important. All these are instances or variations of acedia.

Acedia, the Menace

There's a cunning aspect to acedia: It has an alluring effect in that it attracts certain other afflicting thoughts as well. With acedia, we can soon contend with despondency, which degrades into discouragement or despair. Despair is a deep, death-dealing feeling, suffocating us emotionally and spiritually, and we will address it in the next chapter. Persistent and full-blown acedia leads to feelings of meaninglessness and even intractable pessimism. We may eventually feel that the final verdict on life is only nonsense or absurdity. This is nihilism, and it is the spiritual opposite of dynamism and life. Such a conclusion is a kind of total demise—one that includes abandoning any hope and joy or possibility to give or receive love and goodness.

Acedia relates directly to our relationships with God and others. It threatens us to the core, although it sneaks in as common and nonthreatening things, at first, like dissatisfaction and discontent. Please be aware: Acedia is of a spiritual nature and shouldn't be confused with medical conditions like hormonal issues or chemical imbalance—all of which need professional intervention. It's possible to conflate acedia with one of these issues, in certain instances. If you are struggling and barely getting through life, make sure to see a physician or a mental health professional without delay to rule out a treatable medical issue.

Let's note that acedia stays a devil obscured in paradox and complexity, one that affects spirit and body with a strange listlessness. The confusion is destabilizing and frustrating. It leads to irascibility that nurtures wrath, the elders tell us. Though acedia zaps our motivation and siphons our energy reserves, its worst attribute appears when it stands in opposition to love, which comes from God. Acedia tempts us into isolation.

The Barrier to Love

One way God's love comes to us is in the form of a rescue project to save us from ourselves. We are not meant to fight the battles of life feeling alone or apart from God's love and separated from the care of others. Acedia puts an abrupt stop to that. Acedia erects a barrier to love and spiritual growth. In his book *The Noonday Devil*, author Jean-Charles Nault explains how acedia is a common experience in our culture now. With acedia, we begin to "side-step God" as we "rely on [our] *independence* to satisfy us and we mistakenly equate that with freedom." We soon are disillusioned with finite things, says Nault, and this leads to a classic kind of hostility or disappointment with life. We think we are choosing freedom-giving independence, but we are actually choosing death-dealing isolation.

In our time and context, this also plays out in the continual pursuit of distractions that technology bring us; or in bouncing from one close relationship or romance to the next; or in following trends in gossip, society, news, fashion, or entertainment. We are always looking for the next thing to which we can attach. For more concrete examples, perhaps a writer bounces from one absorbing project to the next without finishing much, because digging deep feels too vulnerable. Maybe a musician feels stuck and spends time enviously following the accomplishment of colleagues, while not finishing their compositions out of acedia comingled with fear. Maybe a spiritual seeker avoids training related to their calling and instead jumps from one vapid project to the next, hoping, somehow, to find satisfaction each time. There are a legion of possible examples. You can probably remember a season of your life in which you felt this way.

We notice our acedia too in our ongoing disquiet or generalized fickleness, or when we experience the feelings of missing out. If we stop to think about it carefully and take a look around, it seems that acedia, in various forms, permeates our times.

How We Persevere Against Acedia

To get a handle on acedia, we can first witness how acedia is confined to a particular place and time. In other words, with acedia we are tempted by frustrations that urge us to escape our present situation. Kathleen Norris says, "[acedia] also sends us backward, prettying the past with the gloss of nostalgia." Sometimes acedia shows up in us as distractibility and sorrow about our place in life. Practically speaking, we contend with this well by doing something challenging but simple, using time and space to our advantage: staying put and riding it out. We allow ourselves to be moved and comforted by the Spirit exactly where we are right now—whether we feel vulnerable or strong.

For many desert monastics, the long days could add up to discouragement. Renowned monk and bishop Palladius of Galatia (circa 363–420 CE), who spent years visiting many of the desert enclaves and sought the guidance of Abbas Evagrius and Macarius, said, "One day when I was suffering from boredom I went to Abba Macarius and said, 'What should I do? My thoughts afflict me, saying (to me), you are not making any progress, go away from here.' Abba Macarius said to me, 'Tell them, for Christ's sake, I am guarding the walls.'"

Abba Macarius encouraged Palladius to not give in to acedia. He advised him to think of every moment of devotion as beneficial, whether it felt that way at the time or not. Macarius teaches that if faithfulness does not feel like progress, then consider vigilance and watchfulness as a way to stay firm in our commitments. The advice about "guarding the walls" is lesson for us to understand that even boring times are useful. This mindset infuses more meaning into what gets monotonous.

And finally, here is some good news: After a victory over acedia, we find spiritual joy and peace, says Abba Evagrius. A grounded sense of acceptance and contentment come once we steer through the affliction of acedia thoroughly.

> Exercise great humility, bear with interior distress; be vigilant and pray often with reverence and groaning, with purity of speech and control of your eyes. . . . Do your work in peace.
>
> —Abba Moses

Acedia and all its friends are foiled by intimacy with the living God and the nourishment of the fruit of the Spirit. It is our abiding faithfulness that withstands acedia. We may also find a potent remedy for our acedia by repenting of it and then finding a deeper understanding of the incarnation. Taking the bread and cup during communion is a profound reminder to us, in ritual and presence, that we ingest the Bread of Life: God, Spirit, and Jesus, who was broken for us.

Together, we partake of a God-infused life of magnanimity; in faithfulness we offer up our praises, pulled from all the glories of the living world. We direct them back to our Creator, Sustainer, and Redeemer. Paraphrasing the apostle Paul, we no longer live—sinfully, alone, and independently—but Christ lives in us and through us (Galatians 2:20). Our greatness is found in Christ, say the desert elders. This new life happens individually, yes, but more importantly, it happens to an entire community—world without end.

> Trust the original desire for connection with God and be fervent in prayer, so acedia will pass.
>
> —Amma Theodora

A helpful way to vanquish acedia is by strengthening our joyful perseverance. This was a quality for which Abba John the Small was famous. One way that can happen is as we remember and meditate on the ways God has already provided for us. One Scripture passage that can hearten us in this process is Psalm 50:12: "Restore to me the joy of your salvation, and strengthen me with a willing spirit." This can be a prayer that is lived out—a practice we keep, a habit we form as we withstand the torments of acedia. "Trust the original desire for connection with God and be fervent in prayer, so acedia will pass," Amma Theodora advises.

As we detach from our pursuits involving ambition, we make space for more protection against the powers of acedia. Instead of attaching closely to our plans or wanting to be entertained or amused as our life unfolds, we hold our expectations loosely. We stop expecting life to be as exhilarating or action-packed as a spy thriller or as enthralling as a bodice-ripper romance novel. In faithfulness, we wait with glad expectation for the presence and quiet comfort of God and the revealing of God's will at the pace that is surely slower than our own.

Lastly, let us guard against acedia because this demon dares to take vitality from us and our relationships. If acedia is unchecked, it can leech the life, goodness, and dynamism from the connections that normally sustain us. We can take measures to strengthen ourselves to "not grow weary in doing good" (Galatians 6:9). These can happen through spiritual practices inspired by desert spirituality or other meaningful exchanges that uplift us. Consider now: What could you begin as a spiritual practice to prevent acedia or overcome it?

Wisdom from Abba John

Now let's hear some wisdom about dealing with acedia that comes straight from Abba John the Small—who surely guided many spiritual seekers with this common struggle. Of persisting in the spiritual life, he advised, "A house is not built by beginning at the top and working down. You must begin with the foundations in order to reach the top. The foundation is our neighbor, whom we must win, and that is the place to begin. For all the commandments of Christ depend on this one."

Relationships of mutuality and selfless acts of "neighbor love" will protect us from the pitfalls and temptations of languishing in afflicting thoughts of acedia. As we make our way, together, we find increased support, camaraderie, and added help for when we are tempted to abandon our course, or the rules and rhythms of life we've committed to enacting.

We cultivate faithfulness and connections to keep an open spirit. If our relationships become anemic, atrophied, or undercultivated, we all are left vulnerable. We can take a quick lesson from nature with the African zebras—or as I like to think of them, flamboyantly dressed horses. Zebras are protected from a hungry lion by the dizzying and confusing zigzag coat pattern movement that occurs as the herd travels together. Stripes on a rogue zebra make it easy prey. Similarly, going off on our own means we miss out on the protection and strength of others. We, too, have been designed to both survive and thrive together. Through that support, we can fend off acedia.

Reflect and Respond

- Are you having any struggles with acedia, or do you notice any around you?
- Do any of the descriptions of acedia strike a chord of familiarity within you?
- What situations, thoughts, or feelings come to mind to consider in prayer and with a trusted person later?

Pray

Scripture Prayer:

> *Restore to me the joy of your salvation, and strengthen me with a willing spirit.*
>
> Psalm 50:12

Consider using this scripture above, or another one you find encouraging, in a sacred reading practice (in Latin, *lectio divina*).

Directions For Lectio Divina

Read: First, read the scripture very carefully and slowly three or four times. Out loud is preferable. Take it in with your whole being.

Reflect: Second, reflect on the meaning of the scripture. Think of what it could mean for you personally. Spend a bit of time mulling it over and meditating on it.

Respond: Third, pray the scripture straight to God, and allow it to be your source of comfort. Ask God to meet you where you are, and be sure to allow for silence and moments of listening in your prayer time.

Rest: Fourth, allow for your prayer to become more silence than words—more waiting and sensing the presence of God than doing and speaking. Spend time imagining or feeling held close to the chest of God and then settling in to truly exhale and rest.

CHAPTER 6

Antony's Successor

Despondency to Hope

> We can handle the insults of men, but we cannot endure the praises of men.
>
> —Abba Macarius the Great (295–392 CE)

Who of us has not lived through moments or seasons of despair? Of discouragement, despondency, or lack of hope? Such afflicting thoughts happen to us all, and the temptation to despair or give up might sneak up on us seemingly out of nowhere. The desert dwellers, who took on years of austerity, were no strangers to the struggle of overwhelming sadness and despair. But the ammas and abbas of the desert encouraged their students to renew their hope, and they gave their students wisdom for doing so. We need this kind of uplifting wisdom too.

Abba Macarius was also called Macarius the Great or Macarius the Elder, because there was another slightly younger abba with the same name who was called Macarius the Younger. Macarius the Great is considered a father of the fathers, with a significant influence on thousands of people directly, Abba Macarius demonstrates for us compassionate and helpful wisdom for hopeless feelings, or times when we want to completely give up. Abba Macarius learned from Antony the Great and was given his staff and monastic habit when Antony died. The passing of the staff and the garment signified a passing of the torch, as the monastic leadership and legacy went on to Macarius. Such an occurrence mirrored the Old Testament story in which the prophet Elijah leaves behind his mantle for his successor, Elisha.

Many of us will encounter hard times for a season. As we think about deep sadness in this chapter, and the despondency that may be its by-product, let's notice how there are different kinds of sadness. What are they? From spiritual mother Amma Syncletica, we learn, "There is grief that is useful and there is grief that is destructive." When normal bouts of sadness common to the human experience linger and wedge us into despair and despondency, we need release from these very afflicting thoughts that can overwhelm us. Some desert elders described such terrible despondency as a "worm of the heart" that can eat into and hollow out its suffering host.

Abba Macarius had a soft heart and wise words of encouragement for suffering seekers. When Evagrius was new to desert life and was struggling with temptations including despondency, he sought the counsel of Abba Macarius. Those in the desert routinely sought the counsel of those further on the spiritual path. In our context, we are less likely to do that and are quick to self-medicate our sadness. We are much more reluctant to seek guidance from spiritual mentors with our quandaries. We can learn from times past that moving through normal periods of deep sadness at a slower pace is far healthier than ignoring it and finding a guide or a companion for spiritual encouragement is crucial.

The Life of Abba Macarius the Elder

Abba Macarius was no stranger to sadness and grief. His life began in an Egyptian village called Ptinapor. He married young, but his wife died early on in their marriage and before they had children. He then cared for his elderly parents until they died. Losing loved ones made his heart tender and compassionate—full of empathy toward others who were struggling and suffering. As a young man, Macarius was keen to live simply and learn ascetic ways. A gracious desert elder living outside his village began to teach him. This man built a hut for Macarius to stay nearby and showed him how to weave baskets, how to fast, and how to pray. After a short time, the elder hermit suggested Macarius move closer to a nearby village, perhaps to be of service to others. Because of his piety, Macarius was ordained a priest in the town, but it was against his will. He wasn't interested in status or the position of village cleric.

Accounts say that around this time, a young woman accused Macarius of impregnating her. Although it was a false accusation, Macarius never defended himself against the charge. Enraged villagers ganged up to mock and beat him. They even strung heavy cooking pots around his neck and paraded him around the town while berating him and saying, "This monk seduced our daughter. Let him be hanged." He endured this without protest. When they finally tired of humiliating him, he asked a friend to sell all his weavings of mats and baskets so the money could financially support the young women who accused him. Though it must have felt like a hopeless situation, Macarius didn't give in to despair. Without bitterness or despondency, he aimed to help her. He worked nonstop for months to send more money her way.

As the story goes, while the young woman was having the baby, her labor became extremely long and painful. She began to feel guilty and grew concerned that her deception about Macarius might be to blame. Exhausted, she confessed her hoax and named the actual father. Soon she gave birth.

The villagers who had been so cruel to Macarius learned of their mistake and regretted slandering and abusing their village priest. They tried to find Macarius to obtain his forgiveness and to sing his praises. But before they could get to him, he left for the desert valley of Natron, about one hundred kilometers northwest of Cairo, in present-day Wadi El-Natroun. There he began his Scete community, at just thirty years old. He continued living in desert until the end of his life at nearly a hundred years of age. A monastic community that is named after him remains there to this day. (Find the Resources section in the back of the book for a link to see it for yourself.)

Many would-be monastics flocked to Scete to live near Abba Macarius and learn from him. These seekers included Egyptians, Syrians, Greeks, Ethiopians, Armenians, Nubians, Asians, Palestinians, Italians, Gauls, and Spaniards. Each built a small dwelling with mud bricks and a thatched roof to live in. These hermitages all surrounded the abba's small cell.

As Abba Macarius became Macarius the Great, he became revered as a legendary spiritual father and wonderworker. All knew him as a gracious and wise elder—a humble, kind leader of his community as it flourished and expanded for many decades.

After about thirty years, Abba Macarius left the community in the hands of Abba Pafnutius and went south, perhaps hoping to retire and gain true solitude. In that new area, he dug a cell out of rock—and he did one better. Within that cell, he also dug a long tunnel to a secret place where he could get away from visitors and have extra solitude and silence for prayer because he sensed that spiritual seekers would likely start to look for him again.

That clever layout was portentous! Soon disciples followed him to this new location and built huts nearby from mud with reed or palm-leaf roofs. Not hundreds but thousands came. During the week, they would spend their days as hermits in their cell huts while they read Scripture, prayed, and worked in silence, sometimes weaving or making rope. On Saturday evenings, they would hear from Abba Macarius the Great, and on Sundays they would gather for liturgical assembly at the divine hours—meaning they met every three hours throughout the day for prayers and readings, and had a specific time for the celebration of the Eucharist. This they called the divine liturgy.

Despondency Combo Pack

Despondency is common but complex, and it can nag at us and afflict us in ways that can lead to complete despair—a loss of hope. Afflicting thoughts of despondency can keep us mired in difficult places emotionally and spiritually. Spiritual despondency shouldn't be confused with debilitating clinical depression or a chemical or hormonal imbalance that can be mitigated with medication under a physician's care. Despondency, as an afflicting thought, is a spiritual malady that keeps us from peace with God. It often presents itself along with other afflicting thoughts, which we can unpack now.

Despondency often arrives as a combo pack of misery—something that involves various plaguing emotions and temptations. A deep but ordinary bout of sadness can slouch toward temptations of despondency that lure us into a pit of wretchedness. To this sad circumstance may come despondency's "plus one"—acedia, in the form of restless emptiness, apathy, or spiritual lethargy. Then perhaps wrath will join in. This is how afflicting thoughts usually work—they bring along cohorts of other afflicting thoughts as they try to, in a sense, claim squatters' rights to us.

> As it is said: "Our God is a consuming fire" (Hebrews 12:24): so, we . . . must kindle the divine fire in ourselves through tears and hard work (devotion).
>
> —Amma Syncletica

But listen (and this part is very important): This opening up of ourselves to despondency does not happen by accident, nor through the sadness concurrent with suffering and circumstances that we will all experience. No. Being *mastered* by this afflicting thought comes by our choice to push away the love of God during our times of intense suffering. It happens when we reject God's comfort. Sometimes we may do this out of a poor habit or a misperception. When we step into the clutches of any of these temptations, we let afflicting thoughts have their way with us—and too often it can happen when we are really at our weakest. Yes. Sometimes in our misery, we actually make an awful mistake and *choose* to be more miserable. We sometimes choose to spurn the love of God and make an agreement with the afflictions to become hopeless—on a conscious level. It's like picking at a scab: We know we shouldn't do it, and we understand that it won't help the healing process, but we do it anyway. Haven't we all chosen to stay gloomy and miserable at times? Even wise figures like Abbas Evagrius, Moses, and Palladius made that all-too-human mistake.

Abba Macarius the Great taught that our free will is strengthened and God is glorified as we obey in devotion, even as we resist convincing temptations like despondency. He said, "In truth, the Lord seeks neither virgins nor married women, and neither monks nor laymen, but values a person's free intent, accepting it as the deed itself. God grants to everyone's free will the grace of the Holy Spirit, which operates in an individual and directs the life of all who yearn to be saved." The elder encourages us to seek comfort and intimacy with God during such struggles.

Desert monastics, when misled by the temptation of despondency, would start to compare their present life—of commitment to the simple and strict desert way—with their previous life, which now seemed preferable. Despondency could find a foothold and dissolve their resolve. These afflicting thoughts could then be followed by envy of those living outside the religious life, who seemed to have it better. All of us may feel a bit despairing at the loss of control that comes from making a choice that requires regular discipline.

Showing us how astute he was to the vulnerabilities of our human inner workings, Abba Evagrius also noticed a second tendency as the demon of despondency intensified: an increasing and sometimes obsessive concern about the lives and virtues of others. In this stage we may grow critical and overly interested in the goings-on of others, even as we become neglectful of our own walk of faithfulness. What a brilliant insight. Perhaps we are trying to distract ourselves from our own misery. In any case, at this stage of despondency or encroaching despair, we can turn to advanced-level nitpicking! Have you ever gotten stuck in this mode? If so, you may know how this descent into faultfinding can create discord, distract us from spiritual growth, and harm others, all while making us feel disconnected from God.

Spiritual Practices That Curb Despondency

According to the elders, there are two categories of despondency that shouldn't be mistaken for each other. We've already spoken about the negative one. But the positive one is the kind of despondency that leads to repentance, which includes generative, godly remorse and willingness to change. It leads to life.

If we sense in ourselves a sadness that is rooted in mourning over our wickedness and mistakes, the elders agree that this is a positive emotion, because by it, we may dare to improve. And the sadness we feel for others who are struggling from wickedness and weaknesses has the same good and hopeful intention. Within these hard feelings of "good grief" we have hope that we (or others) can stop what we are doing and be transformed. Abba Moses might be one of the best examples of this variety of despondency, and Amma Syncletica was well-known for weeping copious tears of remorse. But this quality of sadness that accompanies repentance was common for the elders. This type of despondency reminds us that emotions that *seem* negative can be ultimately beneficial.

Amma Syncletica cautions us that there is also grief that is not good—it comes from the enemy and is meant to disparage and discourage us. We can be thankful that she and other desert elders offer some ideas for dealing with this predicament. She advises that "this spirit must be cast out, mainly by prayer and singing the psalms."

I appreciate that Amma Syncletica includes singing in her recommendation. In our context, we could sing hymns, church songs, gospel music, and songs of any genre that help us cry out to God. The way our lungs fill with air and our bodies vibrate with sound as we sing can connect us to something deeper and more secure than our fluctuating feelings of gloom. We can begin to embody a different way of feeling and fend off temptation to give in to despair or give up our hope.

Fending Off Despondency

Some of our current afflictions of despondency are worsened by our inability to hold space for sadness. We already learned that in ancient times, songs of lament helped people move through periods of grief and misery together. Even in recent memory, people made time to "have the blues" and allow themselves to move through sadness at a slower pace. Blues music sprang up as a response to downcast and troubled people and times, and it allows any singer or listener some space to feel sad—as sad as we need to feel. Singing the blues was all part of feeling well again, and adding music could be a good way to do it. This way, you could take your time with how you felt instead of just shoving it down, running from it, or hiding it. Consider how you encounter sadness. Do you usually hurry past these feelings or try to put on a brave face instead of giving yourself space to feel sad? Many of us do.

Gospel and blues music are the art forms of people who should, by many estimations, have felt hopeless. But they found a way to keep hope alive through awful times of enslavement and subsequent trials. Black gospel music, in particular, has an ingenious way of including the cries of pain and suffering along with carrying in it remedies of hope and fortitude. We can let ourselves be buoyed by the spiritual songs that are also the prayers of the people who persevered through untold suffering. Whether done in congregations as a communal spiritual practice or on the front stoop, such practices work like taking medicine and then putting on armor from God to endure the battles and weather the storms of desperate despair and carry on.

There are plenty of things to be sad about, and it's important to acquaint ourselves with such sad things deeply and fully—just as we are fully human. We have to let the feelings of sadness metabolize so that we can move on properly, which takes more time than we realize.

Abba Evagrius also instructs his students to reorient themselves through scripture. By reading scripture, we can recast our thoughts and affections away from the troubling emotions or attacks, and toward God in a posture of ongoing trust. It is the posture of trust that starts to turn the tide.

Three Theological Virtues

Because despair can feel like sinking steadily in emotional or spiritual quicksand, it helps to know that hope vanquishes despondency. There are as many ways to find hope as there are people who have not given up. The encouragement of others, especially those who are familiar with our struggles, moves us away from the force of gravity that despondency possesses.

Treasure hunting—finding joy and delight in simple but meaningful occurrences—can also leave us with sparks of hope that begin to light our way out of the darkness of the gloom. Letting our laughter flow easily and freely and allowing ourselves the space to laugh, even through tears, can also feel like good medicine. We may also need a cathartic yell to renew our energy and hope.

Peter Kreeft, the author of over eighty books on philosophy and theology and a professor at Boston College, writes that "no mere feeling in itself is virtuous or vicious." We need not feel bad, guilty, or sinful for experiencing any feelings—positive ones or negative ones. What is in our power is to say yes or no to God.

It is with our will's free consent that we give in to feelings, in a sense collapse into them and attach. Such a decision is what makes our choice morally good or evil, Kreeft says. The despair and despondency we are speaking of is not psychological, but theological. To abandon despondency, we must nurture the three theological virtues: hope, faith, and love. When we refuse hope, we find despair.

Ways to Ditch Despondency

To find sustained liberation from despondency, we need a deeper personal understanding of why it arises within us. We can educate ourselves or enter into a therapeutic setting to find healing, but there are no quick or easy answers. As we work through our struggles with the help of the Holy Spirit and other trusted companions, slowly we find traction for scaling such common but formidable obstacles.

Let me also offer some simple spiritual practices that can bring some relief. First, we can prioritize the solace of a healthy community or a support group. Begin to research and ask yourself: Where can I find authentic community in which I can share vulnerably and openly?

Then, with a steadfast prayer practice during attacks of despair, let us remember that we have the opportunity to reimagine the world—co-creating with God new paths forward to life and hope. Abba Macarius offers some simple ways that prayer can guide us. This elder teaches us something that may give us a sigh of relief, saying, "Prayer does not require many words. We only need to say, 'Lord, as you will and as you know, have mercy on me.'" And if the conflict grows fiercer, Abba Macarius says, "Say to God, 'Lord, help!'" There's a prayer that is straight to the point.

This particular afflicting thought that bedevils us is no tiny obstruction. If you've suffered from deep sadness or despair, you are in the company of many saints before you. If it's weighing you down now, be encouraged to carry on. The past, present, and future people of God love you and are rooting for you, and in the end the victory will be all of ours to celebrate together. Don't feel ashamed if hope gets hard to find sometimes. Remember that you are not a stranger to suffering, and you already possess wisdom from trials you've survived and battles you've already won. Recalling our successes can renew our hope. May you gain the courage to forge on with God's help.

Reflect and Respond

* Have you ever wanted to give up hope? What pulled you through?
* Have you ever felt pressure to make your prayers sound a certain way?
* Has your despondency made you feel far from God's care?

- ✳ For a few moments, reflect on how you can ask God for help, simply. Now write out some words of request or thanks to God. Or you could take some notes about your thoughts and feelings from the chapter or about using simple prayers in the future.

Pray

Slowly repeat the prayer Abba Macarius gave us. *"Lord, as you will and as you know, have mercy on me."*

If you are struggling with despondency, you can pray this simple but potent prayer: *"Lord, help my troubled heart."*

Part III

Spirit

CHAPTER 7

Pillars of the Community

Vainglory to Modesty

> The divine word can bear no fruit, being choked by our cares. Let us, then, renounce these cares, and throw them down before the Lord, being content with what we have at the moment; and living in poverty and rags, let us day by day rid ourselves of all that fills us with [arrogance].
>
> —Abba Evagrius

On May 22, 2002, famous endurance artist and extreme performer David Blaine was lifted up by crane seven stories to stand atop a hundred-foot-high pillar in Bryant Park, New York City. He stayed up there on a twenty-two-inch platform, a bit wider than a TV tray, for a shocking thirty-five hours straight. After that exhausting feat he jumped into a pile of cardboard boxes below. What a stunt!

Blaine claims he got the idea from . . . guess who? A desert-dwelling ascetic! A most daring craze took over in certain spots during the desert movement: living atop a pillar. Obviously, desert ascetism was already extreme living by any standards, but as we will learn, sometimes a monastic chose a more stunning way to—literally—stand out from the crowd.

Before we wonder about some of these boundary-pushing ascetics' possible motivations, we can explore the entry point they offer us for speaking about a pernicious temptation that Abba Evagrius said most often plagues people trying to be righteous. It's called vainglory. *Vain*, in this case, means something that is not lasting. It is temporary, meaningless, passing, or ephemeral. And *glory* is recognition. Vainglory is another way to say "superficial recognition." And while vainglory may sound like an old-fashioned term applied in unfamiliar or ancient situations, it is a behavior readily evident in our personal lives and our culture. In fact, vainglory is having something of a renaissance. Showoffs are rewarded now more than ever before.

Pillars in the Community?

The first of these ancient daredevils was Symeon the Stylite, who lived from 390 to 459 CE. He spent at least thirty-five years on his *stylos*, which is Greek for pillar. Yes, I said years. His pillar towered fifty feet atop the mountain of Qal'at Sem'an, near Antioch, Syria. Raised betwixt heaven and earth, like Jesus on the cross, he fasted and he prayed: day and night, in snow, wind, and rain. Imagine if someone in your neighborhood stood on their rooftop, for months on end, in sleet, rain, and snow. News reporters would gather and viral videos would start circulating.

As Symeon began this spectacular display, concerned monks of his community urged him to come down. Then they threatened to drag him off by force. It seemed like a madcap stunt by a fanatic. But was it? Wondering what was happening and if Symeon had risen to lofty aggrandization, the community leaders all came to check on him. When Symeon obeyed them and returned to the ground to speak with them, they sensed his humility. Ultimately they relented to his desire to accomplish this unique, though risky, ascetic practice. They decided he had merely chosen a severe but permissible practice of self-mortification. Symeon was approved to continue living on a pillar as long as he wished.

Accounts indicate that Symeon survived his three decades living fifty feet off the ground with the help of boys who climbed the pillar to bring him drink and bits of food. Some accounts mention that he pulled up bare nourishment by rope. I imagine, his other needs, of the chamber-pot variety, would have been no fun for him, or anyone else, to deal with.

Symeon's pedestal made him widely famous, as you might imagine. Records say that "rivers of pilgrims" came to see him. Remember that most buildings at the time were not nearly this high. Plus, his platform stood atop a mountain and could be seen for miles. Some visited Symeon to marvel, and some asked for a word of wisdom, a blessing, or for a healing prayer. Visiting pilgrims began collecting dirt from the base of his column to take away with them. This first pillar-dwelling hermit incited many imitators, and plenty of them also went by the name Symeon in his honor. The first Symeon is still highly revered in Eastern Orthodox Christianity. His feast day is celebrated on September 1.

Let's pause for a moment to realize that we can't claim to know Symeon's motivations, or anyone else's, for that matter. Ultimately, it's not for us to level a judgment on those participating in the pillar phenomenon of that period. It's between them and God. What we do know is that it's possible for something that begins as a devout practice to get out of control or twisted. We do know that what begins as faithfulness sometimes may be co-opted by others beyond what was intended. We get caught up in the hoopla.

What is known in this standout case is that, as time went on, Symeon's community established a marketplace for keepsakes made from clay that depicted Symeon and others on their pillars. This enterprise supported their community and eventually brought in considerable income. When visitors or pilgrims were traveling through, they could also buy minted souvenirs, known as pilgrim tokens. (If you are curious to see images of artifacts of both clay and metal keepsakes, you can find links in the Resources section at the end of this book.) Following his death, Symeon was buried on the mountain where he had perched, and the site became the center of a sprawling pilgrimage complex.

It wasn't the possibility of being minted on coinage, however, that first inspired Symeon's ascension to new heights. He was once a shepherd who had developed into a strict ascetic and lived in solitary ways for years. As he tended toward the extreme end of ascetism, he had a pattern of picking ever more confining places to live—not up in the air, but down underground: cisterns, wells, and pits. Understandably, he began getting a reputation as one of the more eccentric of the desert hermits. This strangeness attracted curiosity and more followers.

Living in such peculiar places made Symeon more dependent on others than contemporary hermits of his time. He needed others to provide some help, like food and water for survival. As visitors helped him, they would ask him for wisdom, prayers, healing, and blessings. With the growing number of admirers, he lamented how the added attention only distracted him from prayer. That's what prompted his idea of moving upward. Up and out of reach he went, away from the pesky throngs. He became Symeon the Stylite.

Accounts say that Symeon the pillar-dwelling hermit inspired at least fifty copycats, including some women. A number of years later, the trend made it out of the desert and into some places in Europe. At that point some ascetics even adapted the pillar-standing life into a way to squabble. English medievalist Roger J. H. Collins reports that if two or more stylites would find themselves within shouting distance of each other on their respective pillars, they might use the occasion to argue theological differences. Such an occurrence literally goes against everything in the desert spirituality ethos. It's an instance that reveals how some ascetic practices didn't always translate well across culture and time. Moreover, instances of pillar-standing for public quarrelling also remind us that not everything the ascetics do is virtuous and worthy of imitation!

Tales of these extreme desert ascetics would not be complete without the story of stylite child prodigy Symeon the Younger (521–597 CE). Like others, he took the name of the first Symeon. Accounts say that he started pillar-standing literally before he lost his baby teeth, at the tender age of about six. Lil' Symeon first began such intrepid feats by imitating a beloved spiritual father named John, who was a stylite outside his village. The boy would stand on his own smaller pillar near John's pillar. My guess is that people probably thought it was adorable. Mini Symeon likely had encouragement from his mother, which may corroborate that "stage parents" are an ages-old phenomenon. She took her son to live on the outskirts of her city with other ascetics after Lil' Symeon's father died in an earthquake. Stage mom or not, she may have hoped that creating a pint-sized phenomenon as a public display of devotion could help their fatherless little family to survive. They subsisted on the donations from visitors and admirers, and Lil' Symeon went on to be one of the most beloved figures of the time, well after childhood. It seems the disciplined pillar life refined him in many admirable ways.

At the height of this desert-era trend, stylite ascetics became fixtures—landmarks, really. Records indicate that a traveler walking the five- or six-hour route in Syria to the northern ancient city of Cyrrhus, could see various stylites during the whole trip. For all their spectacle, this variety of desert hermit constituted only the minority fringe. And if you didn't deduce it already, pillar-standing could be dangerous. Some got struck by lightning—like Simeon Stylite III. Such calamities can really put a damper on high-platformed practices.

As I've studied the religious fervor that accompanied the popularity of pillar-dwelling hermits, I have wondered, as you must also be wondering by now, What was really going on? Were these ascetics authentically trying to free themselves from continual distractions and the clamor of crowds so they could pray and meditate in greater peace? Or was it attention-seeking behavior? Was their choice of strenuous spiritual practice just a unique selection of ascetical devotion, one that helped them grow close to God? Or were they simply daredevils whose feats of wonder were designed to prompt the awe and esteem of others?

Praise and Glory

If I were to guess, I'd say that some of the stylites were sincere. Maybe some of them were inspired copycats and some people were looking for a way to be seen and feel special. Maybe some were charlatans from the very beginning. I imagine that some began their pillar-perching with noble goals and virtuous aims, which may have shifted over time into self-centered vainglory or continued because of the expectations of others.

I doubt we are much different once we begin to get copious, ongoing attention.

Author and humorist Mark Twain said, "I can live for two months on a good compliment." Many of us relish being noticed and appreciated. Desiring such social approval is a normal human longing, but it can trip us up as we succumb to the temptation to seek praise or credit. We can crave respect and approval so much that doing good acts or doing well can go sideways. In craving appreciation, we can get our priorities out of order.

Jesus speaks about the religious people of his day parading their good works, such as offering up stagey prayers in public, fasting with looks of agony on their faces, or giving to others when everyone could see them doing it. Jesus said that such displays don't help us grow closer to God. They don't make us better people. They are acts of exhibitionism that don't endure. There are many ways we can feel gratified by the regard, admiration, and kudos of others in our day too.

Jesus offers an alternative and tells his followers to pray in secret: Indoors, away from windows and prying eyes, pray in a small interior space (Matthew 6:6). He also tells them to not give away anything by their appearance that indicates that they are suffering during a fast, which was quite the trend at the time. Perhaps most surprising of all, he tells them to give in *secret*, because God sees everything and knows the intent of our hearts.

Imagine that: Getting no acclaim, credit, clicks, or social advantage for being generous! By giving secretly, our kindness is truly centered on the benefit of *others* and more importantly on honoring God. Jesus wants us to avoid opportunities to look impressive and attract attention—even good attention. How's that for counter-cultural?

So how does vainglory arise in our context? Here's one example. Most of us have come across a conversation or a social media post that could be described as a *humblebrag*. It's a seemingly modest or self-deprecating statement or act that brings attention to something good a person is doing. It's a wee bit scheming. For example, instead of doing a good action with no camera in sight, a person might record themselves giving to the needy or doing some extravagant good deed. It may be accompanied with a modest-sounding caption that *appears* demure and thoughtful. If modesty is inauthentic, then it qualifies as vainglory.

Virtue signaling is another contemporary manifestation of vainglory. Signaling virtue happens mainly through doing certain things or expressing sentiments in order to reflect one's moral uprightness, keen social conscience, or superiority for the ultimate purpose of seeming impressive or being accepted. A bumper sticker or "statement t-shirt" will commonly serve as this type of signal. For other examples, a person might ostentatiously demonstrate a moral stance on an issue such as putting up a yard sign that declares a message or making a message out of some action such as flying a certain flag, driving a certain kind of car, or buying certain products. Another person might lob criticism toward people who are doing those very things to signal virtue to *their* allies, in turn. Both are signaling virtue for personal gain but to different audiences. Both want social brownie points or clout.

Simply put: The *signaling* of virtue is not a virtue at all. The temptation of vainglory demands that we publish, as it were, updates about our goodness, however our group defines it. When we do that, the aim is to obtain validation. Conversely, modesty forgoes the social perks and dopamine hits of getting noticed in favor of the private contentment that we find when we do good unnoticed. Modesty is a way to maintain normalcy and avoid being pretentious. This gives God glory. If we grow in grace by doing good, that's really between us and God. It is private gratitude, not showmanship, that happens through the grace of God and spiritual maturity. We undermine our virtue and progress by broadcasting it.

Vainglory can take an even more sinister turn: It can be leveraged like a weapon to draw comparisons with others, perhaps while hoping to look more pious ourselves. For instance, we say things like, "I can't believe they do that! *I* never would." (Sometimes the second part isn't said out loud.) We make other people's lives or decisions the subject of judgment or scrutiny to put them in their place. By consequence, we get a moral high ground or have an upper hand—or so we imagine. It's an ignoble but all-too-common occurrence in our time, especially for religious people or those who consider themselves upstanding.

Virtues Are Not Innate

Virtues are developed through practice. Good virtues come by good habits. Virtues can also be described as habits with the qualities of the fruit of the Spirit: love, joy, peace, patience, endurance, goodness, gentleness, faithfulness, and self-control. Other examples of virtues are courage, empathy, fairness, prudence, honesty, generosity, and compassion. Possessing and naturally acting out these virtues is something we do out of a mature and well-formed spirituality—the theology we live out. Virtues lived out don't tend to offer material or social rewards. The stealthy temptation of vainglory comes as the powerful urge to gain social rewards rather than be content with often unnoticed spiritual ones.

In our context, many for-profit enterprises like social media companies seem to run on twin engines: outrage and vainglory. Aside from incidental benign content—cats being cute, scenes of nature, or cooking tips—outrage and vainglory power many social media posts. If we aren't participating in one kind, then we might be rejoining the other. As we post, we may think, "I'm taking a stand!" or "Check me out!" We might post our outrage about something terrible someone said or did. We might post impressive accomplishments we've achieved, or acts of generosity, because the validation that comes from vainglory feels good—in the moment. This does not enhance our virtue but disrupts it. When we are modest, we don't get caught up in declaring our goodness or act out vainglory.

Similar to some peak performers of the desert, many millions of people in our context have turned online pillar-dwelling into a way of *being* and even a livelihood. Becoming influential is literally called "building a platform," and the entire purpose is to stand out. Vainglory has not just been normalized; it has been completely commodified. It's a quality that executives, brands, agents, and bosses all hope we possess and cultivate so more sales can happen. We are pressured to manipulate the algorithms with vainglory for our benefit.

Ultimately—and perhaps the stylites learned this too—platform-building becomes an empty and exhausting pursuit. Platform-building is an unending effort that grows frustrating and banal. The self-centered social reward that feels pleasing at first becomes something we grow weary from doing, and we suffer dejection for lack of the validation we continue to crave.

Regardless of what we call it in a specific context, being vainglorious means succumbing to the temptation to vie for recognition or attention—usually for being a good person or being impressive. It's a pitfall that doesn't lead to spiritual maturity, because it turns the gift of grace, which we need for spiritual improvement, into self-righteousness. The entire endeavor, though it may have started out as virtuous, becomes self-centered and self-defeating.

Vainglory derails true righteousness. Abba Evagrius taught that it sneaks up on a righteous-minded person unawares. For many do-gooders, the temptation to vainglory is pernicious. We might be thinking that we are merely setting a good example, taking an important stand on a consequential issue, or showing externally how to live rightly, but we are actually exalting ourselves in the bargain. This "low-key grandstanding" can also come out as false modesty and is identified easily by others as the indulgent desire for recognition and praise. Make no mistake, we can see vainglory in others far more easily than we see it in ourselves.

Getting recognized for our gifts, talents, or spiritual achievement can seduce us into basking in the praise or feeling self-satisfied. That temptation gives us the permission to center ourselves in a story as a spectacle rather than center the power and grace of God—God's glory—as the bigger story. Through vainglory, we take over the narrative, forgetting that any spiritual progress comes as a gift of the Holy Spirit and not by our efforts. If we connect our efforts to our goodness, we dismiss the grace that God has given to us as unneeded. From there, it's a short step to pride, which we will cover in the next chapter.

It's easy, and all too human, to get addicted to affirmation and acknowledgment from others. When quietly doing good stops feel gratifying to us, we get tempted to do good loudly. But as our spiritual life slowly shifts—to become about pleasing others rather than about devotion and intimacy with God—it takes a lamentable turn for the worse. This distortion affects us most in that we lose touch with our greater goals and also our humility—the quality that allows us to be most ourselves. Feelings of insecurity will peak and dip wildly as we tangle with the demon of vainglory and become destabilized.

As vainglory takes control, first it involves how we appear to others, but it quickly results in a distorted self-perception. We will find ourselves needy, even ravenous for the notice of others. Whether it's "likes" and "thumbs up" on social media, or getting the approval or recognition we hope for in person or in print, we can feel compromised by the pursuit of appreciation and start to feel like fakes. We may worry that others think of us as shallow or even contemptible, and we may begin to agree with them.

Desert spirituality offers much wisdom that helps us exit these loops into which vainglory confines us. The way of the desert elders can help us assess ourselves honestly but also not get stuck in self-abasement. Looking at what lies behind vainglory gets us started.

> As wax is melted when confronted by fire, so the soul is dissolved by praises and loses its intensity.
>
> —Amma Syncletica

Amma Sarah was a wise hermit woman with a quick wit. Her wisdom and humility were renowned, but few specifics were recorded about her life. Thankfully, some of her sayings have persisted through the ages. Witness her wisdom as she cautions us about prioritizing the opinions or judgments of others and the temptations of vainglory. "If I were to pray to God that all people might approve of me, I would find myself at each one's door, repenting," she writes. "I would pray, rather, that my heart might remain pure towards all, having neither ill thoughts nor judgment regarding anyone."

Desert elders like Amma Sarah knew that getting caught up in the opinions of others is a losing battle. Things like anxiety, envy, burnout, disappointment, wrath, and a host of other negative outcomes result from the torments of the vainglory devil. Amma Sarah understood that we sometimes overvalue what others think of us in ways that dictate our behavior and distract us from pursing holiness.

What Induces Vainglory?

The internal roots most active at the onset of vainglory are insecurity and fear. The temptation comes also as sensing the outside pressure to pad one's reputation. Our authenticity can't be in question, right? What an awful blow if people think poorly of us. "Let's fix that straightaway!" we think. We must manipulate or maintain people's opinions of us because fear and insecurity work through vainglory, and the demons have carjacked us for a rough ride.

What people think of us isn't just none of our business, it's also out of our control. We worship and serve God, and the imposition of the attitudes and assumptions of others are not our problem. These things will distract us from pursuing intimacy with God. Such distractions become terrible setbacks emotionally, mentally, and spiritually. If we know, in good conscience, that we have been living honorably, only God's opinion about us matters. Living into that truth is a habit we must build.

It's clear to us, as we look back from our contemporary vantage point, that too many ascetics were misguided in their stunning feats of austerity; perhaps, at times, it was to appear holy to those around them and convince themselves. A few ascetics are known to have starved to death from denying themselves food. Some got ill or died early because they were cutting themselves off bodily from basic needs while pursuing holiness. I don't think these people made wise choices. God's love can't be bought by our feats of endurance. It seems to me that too many cut off most enjoyment of life on their quest for godliness. Jesus told us that he came so we would have life and have it more *abundantly*—not more austerely.

While zeal can propel us toward a life dedicated to God and goodness, it can also become misdirected. Running ahead of God in harsh or thoughtless zeal, or perching high up on a pillar for years, are examples of good intentions gone wrong, as I see it. Maturity hinges on overcoming the struggles of our wants and desires that distract us from God and harm our relationships. They must center on God and reflect the glory of God rather than our suffering or specialness.

Though severity was common in the desert setting, not every abba and amma was extreme in their asceticism or advised severe deprivation. Some gave voice to living with devotion and discipline in moderation in a simple setting, like Abba Pachomius and his sister Amma Mary did. Do you remember them from chapter 3? The large desert communities they administered enjoyed fruit every day and ingested enough food, like bread and fish, to nourish themselves in healthy ways.

A mature spiritual life will not look like the lives and conquests of famous people who live at the expense of others. It will have restraint. It will show deference to others. Spiritually mature people will be okay with others getting credit. We will be content in opting out of the competition for recognition, pageviews, likes, accolades, awards, and attention.

How Modesty Curbs Vainglory

So how might we best deal with the demon of vainglory? First, the path to thwart vainglory must include a reckoning with ourselves. We must cultivate self-awareness by undergoing honest estimations of our motivations and intentions on a regular bias. We must inquire of ourselves and ask if our ego may be hunting for validation or if we are desiring some sort of elevation above others. Crucial to that inquiry are the aspects of truthfulness, gratitude, and modesty. We may be more familiar with what truthfulness and gratitude are, but what about modesty? Modesty is moderate apprehending of ourselves that does not assign any grandeur to our appearance, manner, or behavior. It's a sober understanding that we are dependent on grace and that, in light of that grace, our merits are not impressive enough to ever showcase. It's a bold and unpopular sentiment for sure.

And here is maybe one of the best-kept secrets of desert spirituality: If we feel humiliated, it is actually a chance to get better acquainted with humility. A mature and humble person is impervious to humiliation. This wisdom saves us from millions of moments of needless shame. A truly humble person is also one who most appreciates grace and seeks out guidance from others for areas of arrogance and then rids those shortcomings from their life.

> A treasure is secure so long as it remains concealed; but when once disclosed, and laid open to every bold invader, it is presently rifled; so, virtue also vanishes once it is known and made public. Just as wax melts in the presence of fire, so also does the soul disintegrate in the face of praises and lose its vigor.
>
> —Amma Syncletica

If we have a tendency to desire credit for doing good, or if we feel the need to look impressive in front of others, we must practice the activity of "keeping some things to ourselves." We can regularly choose not to overshare and pursue a spiritual discipline of *under*sharing, to coin a word. As we move toward true humility, we may even grow to love the idea that we can keep the good actions we do a secret between only us and God—our holy secrets.

Remember to ask, Why is it so important to me to seem impressive to others? What is missing, such that I now want validation from a place other than God? Then ask, What might be a better way to connect deeply with God in this moment instead? Let us cultivate thankful hearts.

We must be well-versed in acts of service and seek out what is ego-demolishing—not that we should beat ourselves up about it all, but we must nurture the qualities in ourselves that keep us flexible and teachable. Let's also avoid situations of hierarchy, partiality, or any related thinking that blocks us from learning from and hearing from others.

Maybe you've wanted credit for something you did, but you never got it—and that irked you. Haven't we all, at some point, felt disappointed this way? Do you post things on social media to signal the moral high ground you stand on or the good deeds you do? What do we do to make sure that people know that we are good? It's time to pump the brakes on all that.

To curb vainglory, find a way within the next few days to *give in secret*. Make a plan now to ensure it happens. Do you know someone in need or maybe an organization that could use some support? It doesn't have to be about the cash value of your gift. It's about giving freely when no personal benefit seems obvious. It's about enacting generosity itself. It could be an encouraging note, a kind deed, or simply a gift that would cheer someone up—like gathering some wildflowers for an elderly friend, making an extra cup of coffee to give away, sharing something from your abundance, or pulling a neighbor's garbage cans back to their house. Whatever you pick, try to keep it a secret. Keep track of what happens within you and how these moments between you and God are developing something new and rich. In your secret plan, consider making this practice a larger theme and routine in your life.

Desert spirituality includes a fearless generosity that is not of this world. It is not a fleeting way of doing good or an economy in which we become worthy by our efforts. By imitating the virtues of the wisest desert fathers and mothers, not only do we free ourselves, but everyone else gets a chance to be freer too in the process. May we learn to sidestep vainglory and embrace modesty so that we become comfortable with our ineffable worth.

Reflect and Respond

* What are some of the ways you have wanted others to notice your good works or your righteousness? We all do this. What does that look like for you?
* Instead of looking for credit from others, in what ways can you embrace the acceptance you already have with the Lover of your soul?

Pray

O, Lord, I give you glory.
Help me to find my value in your love for me.
Protect me from the temptation of seeking
the approval and attention of others.
My goodness is because of your goodness and grace.
May you be glorified in all I do and that I am.
May others see your radiance as I stay in the
comfort and the shadow of your wings.
Give me a humble and generous heart.
Amen.

CHAPTER 8

A Twist of Spite

Envy to Celebration

> Abstain from everything which is contrary to nature, that is to say, anger, fits of passion, jealousy, hatred and slandering the brethren; in short, everything that is characteristic of the old [nature].
>
> —Abba Poemen

I was knocked for a loop when I recently learned that there were actually nine, not eight, afflicting thoughts. John Cassian never wrote about the ninth one when he conveyed the teachings he learned from Evagrius to Christians in the West. Evagrius wrote about envy at a later time.

Around 590 CE, Gregory the Great, who was far more familiar with the total corpus of Evagrius's writings than John Cassian was, reworked the afflicting thought ideas. He made his own list that became known as the seven deadly sins—and there it was: envy. Abba Gregory thought envy was dangerous enough to include in his grouping of sinful vices. He wrote that envy propagates many other kinds of wickedness, saying, "From envy are born hatred, detraction, defamation, joy in the misfortune of a neighbor, and displeasure caused by his prosperity." Sounds accurate to me.

Years after John Cassian left for the West, Evagrius wrote a work called *On the Vices Opposed to the Virtues*, and here he tackles the topic of envy. Wait a minute. Did he speak of jealousy? Or was it envy? And what's the difference, anyway? These words are often confused for each other or even used synonymously. They are closely related, but not the same, and we will cover them both in this chapter.

Discussing this vice is difficult because envy is often accompanied by elements of avarice, wrath, and despondency. They work as co-conspirators against us. In communities, and within individual hearts, envy is a joy killer, the opposite of contentment and gracious charity. Let's dig a bit deeper to understand.

Pangs of Jealousy

We start with jealousy, which is a simpler emotion than envy. It arises when we sense a *threat* to a valued relationship. Jealousy is a common feeling, and even toddlers and animals exhibit jealous behaviors. Our dog may whine or crawl on our laps to regain our attention if we pet another dog. The cat may step on the keyboard and block the screen. A young child might push away an intruding sibling and say, "No! *My* daddy!"

It's not uncommon for adults to sense a pang of jealousy when, for instance, a close friend speaks to us at length about spending time with or deeply admiring a different friend. We might feel jealous of their limited resource of time or attention and feel that we want more of that for just ourselves. God is described as "jealous" in the Bible because the emotion relates to desiring closeness and sensing that the relationship is vulnerable to outside interference. I used to think having that trait made God sound petty. I suppose the writers of those passages wanted to convey how normal it is to feel a potent attachment to those we value. We all feel jealousy at times.

Nevertheless, a perpetually jealous adult who demonstrates possessive behavior may have emotional wounds carried over from the past. Problematic jealousy often involves ongoing feelings of suspicion and apprehension. People who routinely act out of jealousy remind us of children. When adults can't "share" people close to them with others, without it triggering an outburst, emotional dysregulation, or passive-aggressive behavior, those are signs of giving in to jealousy that perpetuates damage.

Once again, let's realize that initial jealous emotions may arise normally, but how we dwell on them or proceed afterward is what makes naturally occurring emotions turn into destructive afflicting thoughts. There are always options for lovingly communicating or renegotiating how and when we spend time with people we care about. We can aim to balance our time in ways that are important to all involved parties. In brief, these are the important elements related to jealousy that speak to our inherent desire to protect what we feel is valuable and threatened.

> My children, desire to purify your hearts from envy and from anger with each other, lest death should overcome you, and you will be counted among the murderers. For whosoever hates his brother, kills a soul.
>
> —Abba Anthony the Great

Green with Envy

Thanks to William Shakespeare's play *Othello*, jealousy has come to be personified in our popular culture as a "green-eyed monster." And maybe you've heard the phrase "green with envy," which stems from the same association. Jealousy and envy are closely related or become mistaken for each other. Envy is also a common, naturally occurring sensation, but in contrast to jealousy, it is most prone to happen within the context of *comparisons*. Envy has more variation and nuance.

Interestingly, we can feel jealousy toward someone we do not envy. The Bible says that God may feel jealous—which involves sensing a threat. But, since God has no equal, God will not envy—and envy can quickly become sinful, which God isn't. As humans, we'd rather admit to being jealous than to admit to being envious. Maybe because envy just sounds nastier? As we unpack it, you'll see how this hunch is accurate.

Because of the element of comparison, the likelihood of envy occurring surges in group settings and therefore in societies. Take note that envy occurs in adults more than in children because it involves more internal reckoning and subtlety. In the case of envy we sense difference, especially our inferiority.

A Twist of Envy

What can start off within us as a positive response—admiration—can lead to a weird twist: envy, and perhaps later to resentment and even hostility. We can struggle with jags of envy that seem to come out of nowhere. To better understand envy, let's realize that it has more facets than jealousy. It's more insidious, highly destructive, and a demon worth defeating.

Rivalries are to be expected in our world, and to be sure, they happened in the desert era too. Of those, historian John Wortley writes,

> A note of rivalry is in fact sounded in the very first lines of the earliest of the Christian monastic documents known to us, *Athanasius's Life of Antony*. The preface of this work (addressing some monks whose names have not survived) begins thus: "It is a good contest-for-superiority in which you have engaged with the monks of Egypt, setting out either to equal or to surpass them in your ascetic quest for virtue." Athanasius is, of course, applauding their enthusiasm rather than inciting them to invidious competitiveness.

It's easy to understand how competitiveness can happen in ascetic religious settings in the same way any group of dedicated people can grow competitive. Desert-dwelling monastics emulated the committed athletes in training who were described in Pauline epistles (1 Corinthians 9:27). They learned these passages and held them dear. With this context, it's no surprise that relationships or occasions might turn from camaraderie into situations of envy. These were thwarted by spiritual wisdom that brought them back to reality and kept them humble.

In the *Evergetinos*, a collection of wise sayings and short accounts from the early monastics, we read that the desert elders encountered situations to which many of us can relate. Here's an example: Maybe somebody makes an argument or asserts a contention—perhaps even a brilliant one. Then, as we interact with it, we want to create a good rejoinder; but, we are actually motivated out of a sense of inferiority. That's envy.

When such a situation unfolded in a conversation with two abbas, here's how they encountered it:

> Abba Ammoun asked Abba Sisoes, "When I read a holy book, my thoughts urge me to compose a fine discourse, that I might have it as a reply when I am questioned. What should I do?"
>
> Abba Sisoes answered, "There is no need for you to occupy yourself with such things. Rather, struggle that, by means of the purity of your mind, you might acquire spiritual calmness and tranquility from on high; and also wisdom from on high, that you might speak and answer in a soul-profiting way."

The wisdom offered in this account advises the brother to let the feelings of envy and competition pass. Keep your ideas to yourself at first, and allow the struggle to purify you so you can acquire tranquility that comes from God and keep your peace, says Abba Sisoes. Then craft your response in a way that will be most beneficial and not just sourced in the urge for rebuttal. With the afflicting thought of envy, we may be tempted into unprofitable competition that harms our peace and disrupts community harmony—because we have decided to center our insecurity and respond from that place.

Sometimes someone else's displays of vainglory get under our skin and trigger envy. We get an itch to respond or clap back. That's when those green shades of envy come creeping over us as we get irritated, perhaps because they point to something we feel insecure about or threatened by. Maybe we envy the admiration someone else receives, the credit someone gets, or an accomplishment they achieve, and with that realization comes some acute sense of our inadequacy—and all of a sudden we feel envy like a harsh tug. Can you think of a time when you felt this way? Most of us encounter plenty of opportunities for potential envy to arise.

> To throw yourself before God, do not measure your progress, to leave behind all self-will—these are the instruments for the work of the soul.
>
> —Abba Poemen

Abba Poemen said that when we are tempted to draw comparisons, whether out of envy or some other reason, we should inquire of ourselves, "Who am I?" We should untangle from our habits of unhealthy comparison and thinking of others' achievements as a personal slight. He says plainly, "Do not pass judgment on anybody." Instead Abba Poemen advises us that protecting each other, not descending into rivalry, expands grace. He says it this way: "At the moment we cover up our brother's fault, God covers up ours, and whenever we reveal the brother's fault, God reveals ours."

Holding negative opinions or envy-based grudges keeps us locked in sinful bargains of envy. When we diminish the success or goodness of others, we fall under envy's toxic spell. Elders taught their students to expel envy from their hearts, immediately. The New Testament book of James says that envy causes disorder and every vile practice (James 3:16). The desert elders took this verse very seriously.

Author Carol Ruvolo describes envy with astute clarity: "frustrated self-exaltation fueled by animosity, resentment, and defensiveness." What an incriminatory diagnosis. Add to that the fact that sometimes we don't realize that envy comes from the negative and all-too-normal emotions of feeling left out. The root of this insecurity is something we can investigate gently with ourselves as we bar it from stunting our maturity.

A father of the church (210–258 CE), Cyprian, who was the bishop of Carthage and was martyred in the period shortly before the desert era, encountered the topic of envy with great thoroughness and wisdom in his writings. There must have been a pressing problem in his setting for the subject to necessitate so much of his time. In his piece called *Treatise 10*, he tells readers how important it is to know where jealousy and envy come from, and how they begin to take hold. He warned that envy should be guarded against more than anything.

> Whoever he is whom you persecute with jealousy, can evade and escape you. You cannot escape yourself.
>
> —Father Cyprian of Carthage

Wishing Ruin

How sad to think that a Christian community that ought to be known for their love can turn into a group of people who root for or begin to enjoy the misery or devastation of others. People stuck in envy may display this distressing trait like a flashing sign. When we are sinning with envy, we find it difficult to rejoice in the successes of others. We may feel like we've lost something when another ends up with a win. Gone is our ability to rejoice when others rejoice and mourn when they mourn.

In our context, some specific, ordinary thoughts that pop up for us might include envying the new car someone else can afford, or the new opportunity, job prospect, relationship, vacation, fitness level, or accomplishment. If someone gains something we desire, or they are put in a position or place we wish we were in, from a point of envy, we will think, "Do they *really* deserve it? Are they any better than me?" We grow disheartened as the envy-based comparison diminishes how we feel about ourselves. Along with envy, the afflicting thought of despondency can then bear down, and oppressive feelings of dejection or discouragement, too. Envy often brings with it other temptations and afflicting thoughts like avarice, wrath, acedia, vainglory, and pride. Envy pushes us to give in to a fear-based mentality, and we begin to act out of anxious scarcity. We get stingy-hearted—thinking and acting like there is not enough to go around. As envious people, we find it hard to form close friendships without envy interfering.

Another unhappy consequence of the demon of envy is the propensity to malign or gossip about others. We can all too easily inflict social punishment, reputational sabotage, or disparagement on the person we envy. We might go as far as gathering people against a person we dislike from feelings that began as envy. Toward the person directly we may use flattery but then speak poorly about them when they are not present. We will grow easily offended by them, even hostile, and our ensuing resentment often propagates anxiety or even, eventually, paranoia. Such things work as a malignancy in a community and inflict lasting damage. Let us pause for a moment of internal, honest inventory to locate any patches of envy that exist currently in our thoughts or relationships so we can ask for God's direct healing.

> It is a calamity without remedy to hate the happy.
> —Father Cyprian of Carthage

Sink into these heartfelt thoughts from Abba Cyprian as you begin to sense how envy may have taken hold of places in your life or in your community:

> But what a gnawing worm of the soul is it, what a plague-spot of our thoughts, what a rust of the heart, to be jealous of another, either in respect of his virtue or of his happiness; that is, to hate in him either his own deservings or the divine benefits—to turn the advantages of others into one's own mischief—to be tormented by the prosperity of illustrious men—to make other people's glory one's own penalty, and, as it were, to apply a sort of executioner to one's own breast, to bring the tormentors to one's own thoughts and feelings, that they may tear us with intestine pangs, and may smite the secret recesses of the heart with the hoof of malevolence.

Father Cyprian is careful to advise about just how self-defeating envy and jealousy can be. The poison directed toward another comes back double on us, as the envious person. The negative emotions have serious and lasting consequences. He calls it a "calamity without remedy" to loathe someone because they have found joy. That should prick our conscience.

Coveting

Envy begets coveting. The latter doesn't exist without the former. One of the Ten Commandments tells us "Do not covet," and too few of us have realized that the problem of coveting comes directly from insidious envy we let run wild within us through making comparisons and feeling insecure. Coveting happens by choice. When we stew on others' blessings or good fortunes and consider them a personal detriment, that's when the sin of coveting can take hold. We misplace our desire.

In the desert era, many would visit the desert and overly admire the devoted people there. But at times, that regard could sour into envy. Feelings of neediness, want, and scarcity would surface to reveal that God was not the source of deepest regard for that seeker. Humans struggle with envy no matter what time period they live in.

Envy makes us competitive in unhelpful and unhealthy ways. It pushes us into one-upmanship. Beyond that, it thrusts us toward unnecessary conflict. It disturbs harmony.

Abba Longinus, who lived sometime in the fifth century, was known as a spiritual father who was quick to give forgiveness. He knew the way to help someone correct their ways was only by gracious tenderness, not by shaming them. The story goes that some monastics were conspiring against another to have him expelled. They dogpiled him when he faltered and confronted Abba Longinus with the problem. Notice how the abba opposed their tactic.

The record of it says,

> Once, when a particular brother had sinned, a number of the elders in the community approached him and wanted him to expel the fallen brother. Longinus, having great patience for the man, knew that it was in kindness and tenderness that the man would find repentance, refused to expel him. Instead, he rebuked the elders that had come to him, saying, "Woe to us because we

renounce the world and have entered into the monastic life saying, 'We are like angels,' but in reality we are more evil than unclean spirits!"

Spiritual Practices to Curb Envy and Jealousy

If we make the time to hold our envy at a distance and examine it, we can look carefully enough at the focus of our envy to help us identify what we are actually passionate about. Instead of faulting another person for having what we want, we begin to know ourselves better and realign with our passions more accurately. They can show us the goals we admire. That can happen without descending into vexation toward another or hatching petty envy.

To curb our tendencies to capitulate to envy, we can begin to deeply apprehend and deeply appreciate that our cup is already full. The spirit of charity counteracts envy. The spirit of celebration will brighten the acrid and turbulent disposition that envy inflicts. Think of how you felt when someone rejoiced in your accomplishment or happiness. Just as we enjoy when others are happy in our successes and joys, let us also realize how beneficial it is to be full of gladness when others have occasion to be glad. Embrace joy when others succeed.

Content people do not envy. Those without envy do not suffer from insecurity or arrogance. They don't act trifling or seem to need validation. They possess a modest and gracious humility of spirit devoid of judgment toward others. They have a sense of assuredness that envious people lack.

> Just as a corpse does not feel anything or judge anyone, so the man who is humble of mind cannot judge anyone, even if he should see him worshipping idols.
>
> —Abba Longinus

Even though envy was not one of Abba Evagrius's original eight afflicting thoughts that he taught to John Cassian, the many years of desert life taught Evagrius that envy was a common demon that plagued spiritual seekers and monastics. That was true then, and it most certainly is true now. Whether deforming our perception or damaging our attitude, envy and jealousy stand out as vices that we can oppose through enacting gratefulness and celebration.

The victories of others do not diminish us. We can start small and begin to add up the ways we are grateful for those we may normally envy. We can anticipate being happy for someone when they succeed because these emotions have a way of becoming a contagious reality in us and to those around us. Generosity begets more of its kind.

Enact celebration to thwart envy and notice the triumphs of others. Express some acknowledgment that you realize would be nice to hear. Live generously and be lavish with blessing, praise, and good wishes. Bouts of insecurity and feeling left out can happen to any of us, and we may never be entirely free of them. But with a continually maturing intimacy with God, who loves us exactly as we are, we can become gracious and joyful people who find new ways to enjoy and celebrate the wins of others without experiencing debilitating envy.

Reflect and Respond

* As you inspect your heart, who have you admired? Who have you envied? Where is envy stealing from you now?
* Take some time to repent and to readjust to center joy and celebration for others as a major feature of your life moving forward.
* List a few ways you will counteract what you've thought or done out of jealousy or envy. How can you build people up and encourage them?

Pray

O, Lord, I am grateful that my cup runs over with your blessing.
When I don't feel I have enough, remind me of your lavish gifts to me.
Forgive my jealousy and envy. Clear my conscience.
Give me a heart filled with gladness for the successes of others
That rejoices in their happiness, that more joy may abound.
Let the celebration of my heart bring you joy and glory.
Amen.

CHAPTER 9

The Final Delusion

Pride to Humility

> The demon of pride conducts the soul to its worst fall. It urges it: First, not to admit (to having) God's help; second, to believe that the soul is responsible for its own achievements; and third, to disdain [others] as fools because they do not [understand].
>
> —Abba Evagrius

We've already been introduced to Abba Evagrius, the desert elder we have to thank for helping us understand the nine afflicting thoughts. As we look into the final demon that plagues us, pride, it's time to learn more of his story and his fraught journey to the desert life.

Evagrius of Ponticus was born in Ibora, modern-day Erbaa in Tokat Province, Turkey, into a Christian family. Early on, Evagrius was well-educated and moved around in the company of famous and influential people. He received acclaim for his mental prowess and his zest for vigorously defending against church heresies. First, he was ordained as a reader in the church for Basil the Great, and he also served as a reader and was later promoted to deacon under Gregory Nazianzen, who was then installed as bishop of the city of Constantinople. Constantinople (now Istanbul) had been the capital of the Roman Empire for more than fifty years by that point. At the first Council of Constantinople in 380 CE, Evagrius was by Gregory's side to settle a major controversy of heresy in the church. That heresy is called Arianism—the claim that Jesus was a created being and subordinate to the Father, rather than begotten and coequal with the Father.

Just two years later, Evagrius became the archbishop. In 381 CE, he accompanied Emperor Theodosius I at the Second Ecumenical Council, which determined the Nicene Creed among other things. So if it's not already evident, let me assure you: Evagrius of Ponticus was a big shot. Quickly, he was swept into the bougie life of the big city and the praises of many admirers. But soon, he became entangled in a steamy infatuation with an elite—and already married—noblewoman, who was gaga for him too.

Even though he escaped the scene for Jerusalem, his conversion to a new and holy way of life was not an immediate one. For starters, he hid the whole scandal from his host, Amma Melania, while staying as her guest at her monastery at the Mount of Olives. At this stage, his qualities of being forthright and prudent were, we might say, aspirational.

Likewise, instead of demonstrating any curiosity about or interest in understanding monastic life there, he took in the sights and sounds of the intriguing Holy City. His wealth and status afforded him perks, like keeping an extensive and fancy wardrobe of outfits—two clothing ensembles for each day in a time when many people owned one or two garments in total.

Evagrius habitually dolled himself up in dazzling attire and strolled around the busy city. A wealthy, youngish, and handsome man, Evagrius knew such a display would create a lavish spectacle of elite style, class, and status.

So Evagrius sashayed around town and languished aimlessly like this for a time, until he became terribly ill. His sickness lasted for six brutal months. Visiting doctors couldn't help him. Finally, after an inquiry by his gracious host, Amma Melania, Evagrius revealed his salacious backstory: his passion for a married woman, hers for him, and her jealous husband who was plotting his demise. Amma Melania advised him to cast off his old life—much like discarding a fancy and cumbersome garment, it seems to me—and take the monastic vows to enter into a life of simplicity, austerity, and humility. She promised to spend time in prayer for him.

So the swanky, runaway archbishop took her counsel and stayed on at the monastery to learn. His life of posh perks, acclaim for his capabilities, and being the center of religious circles and privileged power in the company of the emperor in the capital city was over. But he still had a lot to learn and many devils to overcome.

After a time, Evagrius left Melania's secluded monastic community in the Mount of Olives for the desert life. Out in the desert, the wise Abba Macarius the Great was his closest spiritual father. He guided Evagrius in fending off his many demons and helped him adjust to ascetic life so he could grow in holiness.

Evagrius recounted an interaction with Abba Macarius when he first came to the desert. He wrote, "I visited Abba Macarius and said to him, 'Tell me a word so I may live.'"

Tell me a word: This was a typical thing to say to a desert elder who was your spiritual father or mother. After receiving a "word"—which was a short, wise message—the student would carry it deeply, meditate on it, pray about it, and allow it to change them. After a time, the student might go back for another word or to ask their elder a question or inquire about a concern.

Evagrius continues his story:

> Abba Macarius said to me, "If I speak to you, will you listen, and do it?"
>
> I said to him, "My faith and my love (for God) are not hidden from you."
>
> Abba Macarius said to me, "Truly, I lack the adornment of virtue; you, however, are good. But if you cast off the pridefulness of this world's rhetoric and clothe yourself in the humility of the (contrite) tax collector (Luke 18: 9–14), you will live."
>
> When he said these things to me, all my thoughts dissipated, and when I asked his forgiveness, he prayed over me and dismissed me. And I walked and found fault with myself, saying, "My thoughts were not hidden from Abba Macarius, the man of God, and every time I go to meet with him, I tremble on account of his ability to make me listen and it's a humbling experience for me."

Evagrius was learning straightaway about the demon of pride from Abba Macarius. He stayed on in the desert and continued to learn from a number of spiritual mentors, and he began a life of severe ascetic restraint. While living the rest of his life as a desert hermit, he also spent time translating documents and writing his own work. He eventually became revered for much different reasons than he had as the chief smarty-pants in the capital city: wisdom. Best of all, Evagrius tenderly taught and wrote invaluable guidance for other spiritual seekers, with particular sensitivity for those suffering from temptations to which we all succumb.

Abba Evagrius's giftedness at noticing what hindered spiritual seekers, and his understanding of the inner workings of people, make him one of the most compassionate and astute elders of that or any era. Many ages before psychology would be considered a field of study, Abba Evagrius was revealing, in incisive ways, how our inner vulnerabilities create obstacles to righteous living and harmony with others.

Descent to Madness

Abba Evagrius cautioned that the demon of pride within us is followed by three wretched results: anger, sadness, and utter insanity and madness—"visions of mobs of demons in the air," as he also put it. In our times, we might call that paranoia.

Perhaps unexpectedly, Abba Evagrius defines pride not primarily as conscious, haughty rebellion, which we might typically consider pride to be. This common understanding of pride has also been attached to notions of *original sin* over the years, as that dogma developed. It may be for this reason that later Pope Gregory I (540–604 CE) listed pride as one of the seven deadly sins; he thought it was the most pernicious and wrote about rebellious pride.

Evagrius witnessed pride happening differently in spiritual seekers, however. He saw pride expressed not as overt conceit or rebellion. It's often a more insidious situation. Pride, Evagrius suggests, is better understood as soul-sick delusion. Abba Evagrius noticed that the demon of pride works on us in reverse. Instead of thinking we are choosing to do what is sinful, we feel more righteous than others as we give in to temptations of pride. Through pride, we become unteachable and unreachable. Pride cuts off access to humility so we thoroughly lose our way. Evagrius doesn't see pride just as a pesky issue but as a vicious trap with the potential to ruin us. To progress in virtue and to enact any fruit of the Spirit, Abba Evagrius and the desert elders are univocal in saying that humility is the way to becoming free from pride.

> Humility leads the intellect into right knowledge, drawing it upward, for it is written, "He shall teach the humble their paths." [Ps 24:9]
>
> —Abba Evagrius

Amma Syncletica advises her students about obtaining humility in the context of community, "As long as we are in the monastery, obedience is preferable to asceticism. The one teaches pride, the other humility." Obedience to an abbot or abbess is a way to change the focus from one's individualized, self-centered, or self-pleasing pursuits and accomplishments in holy living. Getting good at the monastic lifestyle will often make a person feel too pleased with themselves, this amma knew. Many of us find that living for God can sneakily turn into an ego project, just like worldly pursuits might, efforts such as completing advanced education, garnering career achievements, finding fame, or gaining wealth.

The desert elders knew that accomplishing severe asceticism can make a person feel self-satisfied and more advanced compared to the beginners. Therefore, submission in the form of obedience becomes a test of one's willfulness and level of humility. To remove ourselves from the top positions and stay obedient students is a way to subdue our pride. The test of submission shows us whether our righteousness is authentic or just another pursuit stemming from a hidden agenda or ego project—whether purposeful or unconscious. It brings to light if humility is truly in us and cultivates humility within us if it is missing.

> Humility protects the soul from all the passions and also from every temptation.
>
> —Abba Dorotheos

In our context, it's seldom that we *willingly* submit ourselves to others in spiritual or other kinds of obedience unless it is absolutely necessary. Who among us wants to be bossed around, right? Yet such situations—of healthy submission—are important for learning who we are. Ask the following: Under whose authority or accountability do I willingly put myself? Whom do I obey? Whom do I learn from? If the list is nonexistent or contains just a few, we stand to succumb to the demon of pride—or else we are already in its clutches unawares.

Just as importantly, we must be careful to not submit ourself to a leader who is not humble—one who demands to be obeyed or grandstands. This goes too for a system or structure that lacks a balance of power, accountability, and transparency. Domineering leaders who act without accountability or who answer to no one are prone to deception from the devil of pride, and they are prone to manipulate others. In them, we will find stubborn arrogance, harshness, and self-righteousness. Want to defeat the demon of pride? Find a humble, unassuming guide and tell them your quest. If they are reluctant to accept your submission to them, you may have found a good one.

Pride Destroys a Community

The elders knew that pride topples leaders and hurts our individual spiritual growth. But Amma Syncletica's wisdom reveals how pride can deeply hurt entire communities of faith. Stealthily, it slithers in, even into the lives of seasoned Christians and monastics, so that righteousness becomes weaponized and a certain noxious competitive or comparative culture develops. This also creates demons of despondency in beginners who become discouraged, said the amma.

This is how Amma Syncletica put it: "On the one hand, with accomplished and ascetic monastics, he [the devil] tries to cover their sins and to make them forget them, so as to create pride in them. On the other hand, he constantly exposes the sins of neophytes, whose souls have not yet been strengthened in the ascetic life before them, exaggerating these sins, so as to drive such neophytes to despair, until they abandon their ascetic efforts."

Progress in virtue puffs us up before we even know it. As abbess of a large community, Amma Syncletica knew well what could create discord and schisms. If we feel more godly than others, if we begin finding faults in others, or if we start comparing ourselves against those who don't measure up to godliness in the way we think it should look, we slip into a pernicious misperception of grace: pride. How easy it is to get overly satisfied with ourselves. We get mistaken notions—thinking we have made virtuous achievements, or other progress, by our gifts, aptitude, cleverness, or talents.

How easy it is to forget who we really are: ordinary sinners who need forgiveness; permanent students of Jesus who need to continually repent, just like anybody else. When this kind of arrogance hardens, we cannot sense the guidance of the Holy Spirit to influence us. We cannot exude the grace and compassion that reflects the kind that we have been given. It is full-blown spiritual sickness.

> Neither asceticism nor hardship, nor any kind of toil, saves, except for genuine humility.
>
> —Amma Theodora

An unknown-to-us desert elder once taught, "Every time a thought of superiority or vanity moves you, examine your conscience to see if you have kept all the commandments, whether you love your enemies, whether you consider yourself to be an unprofitable servant and the greatest sinner of all. Even then, do not pretend to great ideas as though you were perfectly right, for that thought destroys everything." This elder recommended a remedy for pride and feelings of righteous superiority: Take an inventory to get a true account of your shortcomings and realize you need to think of yourself as a flawed learner.

Our practices of righteous living or even of self-denial must never trick us into believing that we are better than anyone else.

Spiritual devotion must never make us think or behave in ways that somehow suggest that God is happier with us or loves us more because of such things. All of us still fall into sin, and pride is one of the most cunning ways it happens.

> For just as it is impossible for a ship to be built without nails, so it is impossible to be saved without humility.
>
> —Amma Syncletica

All of us ought to aim to be contrite sinners, not oblivious ones. We do this while remembering that we are beloved children who may come to God, humbly. We are forgiven through the work of Jesus; that should make us *more* humble and gracious to others, not less. Always consider humility as more than a disposition. It's not like a personality trait that you either have or you don't. Humility is an ongoing exercise of self-restraint.

Too often, religious people give off airs that they are morally better than others, undercutting the very premise they suppose. The desert elders repeatedly tell us this way of thinking and behaving is a terrible trap that harms individuals and communities.

Here's a desert story all about it:

> An unknown-to-us desert abba was asked, "What is humility?" and he replied, "Humility is a great work, and a work of God. The way of humility is to undertake bodily labor and believe yourself a sinner and make yourself subject to all."

> The [student] inquired further and asked, "What does it mean, to be subject to all?"
>
> The abba answered, "To be subject to all means to not to give your attention to the sins of others but always to give your attention to your own sins and to pray without ceasing to God."

Defense Against Pride

From the desert elders, we know that pride will also affect groups and communities, not just us as individuals. The habits of cliquishness, faultfinding comparison, judgmentalism, and any lack of compassion or humility indicate entanglement in pride. Few things are more unloving and un-Christlike. We must repent of those things.

> Humility and the fear of God are above all virtues.
>
> —Abba John

Pride may be the hardest devil to root out in our communities and in our hearts, because we can assume we are living lives of righteousness. We are surely in "God's camp" and not like other people, who live however they want to. Nevertheless, this stubborn demon who leads from the shadows must be overthrown. Our lives should reflect loving humility, meekness, and compassion with no keeping track of how good our progress is or how badly others measure up.

The Jesus Prayer

We've now covered all the major afflicting thoughts. It's time to flesh out more of what life in the desert was like. The day-to-day spirituality that sustained the elders had a foundation we will try to better understand. In the next chapter, we will also delve into the questions that might remain. How can we map the desert elders' spirituality onto our context so their teachings will bear more fruit in our lives? What is the best way to carry their wisdom with us in the contemporary world?

One of the classic elements of desert spirituality is the Jesus Prayer, a short prayer that can be embraced deeply and prayed repeatedly throughout the day. We'll engage with it again at the end of this chapter. But as we contemplate how we might begin to walk in faith inspired by the way of the desert elders, this prayer becomes an important anchor point.

Many millions of people say the Jesus Prayer each day, and countless millions more have prayed it over the ages. The desert elders often uttered it as they worshiped God as a prayer of humility and repentance. Rooted in the prayer of the repentant tax collector in Luke 18:13, it is one of the most common prayers from early Christianity. Abba Evagrius, the desert fathers and mothers, and most spiritual seekers in the desert prayed it often throughout the day in solitude as they submitted their lives in greater devotion.

The earliest *written* reference to this prayer practice modeled after the Luke passage may be in a discourse from desert Father Abba Philimon (from the sixth or seventh century). Also called the Prayer of the Heart, it is held in a collection of writings and teaching of the Eastern Orthodox tradition called the *Philokalia*. We know about the prayer not just from oral and written records but also because ruins of a cell from the desert period in the Egypt have the Jesus Prayer inscribed inside.

Here's one more important suggestion before you get into reading the chapters in part IV: You may want to pick an elder to be your guide as you move forward. (Check the Resources section at the end of this book for a link to help you select one.) Now, reflect on which pieces of wisdom in the book have resonated most deeply and met you where you are. Do any ammas or abbas presented inspire you? Did any elder struggle in the particular ways that you have? Note some ways can you imitate them in virtue. Take their wisdom to heart, roll it over deep within yourself, and ask God to open you up to new ways of learning and growing that will change you into the person you'd like to become.

Reflect and Respond

- What situations or relationships might involve your hidden pride right now?
- How did the person of Jesus show a truly humble example as the incarnation of God?
- How will you now renew your commitment to dethrone your pride?

Pray

Now it's your turn to pray the Jesus Prayer. You may want to pray it as a prayer of repentance—on repeat—until your heart is supple before God and others. Here are some variations:

As Macarius the Great would say it: "God, be merciful to me, a sinner!"

Another common wording: "Lord Jesus Christ, son of God, have mercy on me a sinner."

You may also wish to say it as a breath prayer, inhaling on "Lord, Jesus Christ," and exhaling on "have mercy on me, a sinner."

Some people add the phrase "Son of God" after "Lord, Jesus Christ," and some skip that part.

My favorite alternate version is one I came up with to help me grow in greater intimacy to God's goodness: "Lord, Jesus Christ, have mercy on me, your child."

Part IV

The Ways of the Desert

CHAPTER 10

Intimacy with God

Toward Preventive Spiritual Medicine

> One cannot escape temptation by simply running away. You cannot flee it; you must fight it. We may think that by running away and relocating to a new place, we can rid ourselves of temptation, but we can't.
>
> —Amma Matrona

The way of the desert elders gave spiritual seekers the chance to cultivate the most potent spiritual practices and virtues. This cultivation happened mainly through stillness, silence, prayer, scripture reading and recitation, humility, hospitality, confession with tears, and the remembrance of God and mortality. As they saw it, all the extraordinary things like wonderworking, healing, visions, and ecstatic experiences came in at a distant second place to the primary virtues.

Here in this final section of the book, we will explore desert ways beyond those connected to the nine vices and virtues. We will dig into the teachings of Evagrius on repentance and prayer and take note of his method of encouraging spiritual formation. We will also go more deeply into the specific themes that formed the ways of being for the desert dwellers and transformed them into Christlikeness.

We will begin by learning more about a spiritual mother we read about in chapter three, Amma Matrona, who is unfamiliar to many of us in Western Christianity. As you read and begin to practice walking in the way of this desert elder, may you find yourself being strengthened by her words.

Amma Matrona

Amma Matrona was born around 425 CE and was a contemporary of Ammas Theodora, Melania the Elder, Syncletica, and Sarah. She came from the Roman frontier city of Perge and was educated and wealthy. She moved to Constantinople and married a man named Domitianus and had one daughter, Theodote. She then began to live a more ascetic life and was helped by devoted women, Susanna and Eugenia. She copied their ascetic practice of giving up common beauty standards and instead wore men's clothing and cut her hair short. Her fervency upset her husband, so she ended up fleeing him and giving her daughter to Susanna to raise.

Disguised as a man, she entered a monastery under the name Babylus. After her identity was discovered, she was helped by the abbot Basinas to enter a women's community in Syria and was made an abbess. But her husband eventually found her, and she fled once more to the ruins of a pagan temple near Beirut to live in seclusion until her husband's death. There she had gained a following, so she returned to Constantinople with some of her followers, where she bought an estate and started a women's monastery. This community accepted women of any social class, as visitors or members, and grew into a large and thriving establishment known as a place of learning, healing, and prayer.

Remembering

For Amma Matrona, keeping the memory of God in one's heart and mind and remembering the transitory nature of our human lives are what ultimately still the heart into rest. The habit of bringing to mind the recurring memory of God's love, grace, and goodness and the remembrance of our mortality put into perspective and proper order all that our mind might waywardly wander toward. *Remembering* is a potent way to embrace God's faithfulness.

In the Scriptures, we see a number of prophets cajole the people of Israel to interact with God in this way. The many feast and festival days in the Jewish calendar are all ways the Jewish people gather and remember not just who they are, but what God has done. If you'd like to remember Amma Matrona and the glory she gave to God by her life, you can do so on her special day: March 27. We can use special days—in the church calendar or in our own spiritual or personal calendars—to feed our hearts with remembrance.

> My Lord said to me: Do My work and I will feed you; but do not scrutinize from where it will come.
>
> —Amma Matrona

Repentance Is Vital

A key lesson we learn about ourselves from the desert elders, especially Abba Evagrius, is that temptation and sin are common issues all humans deal with, and they are best dealt with prior to them happening at all. You might say that Abba Evagrius was a "preventive specialist" of sorts, rather than a police officer enforcing the law, a prosecuting attorney, judge, or jury when it comes to dealing with sin. Remember: He does not believe in the later doctrine of original sin that assumes we are 100 percent wicked at the point of conception. Abba Evagrius understands the internal vulnerabilities of spiritual seekers that all humans share. It is with a combination of grace, compassion, and fatherly firmness that Abba Evagrius teaches the spiritual disciplines we need to be sustained and transformed.

Because we are so vulnerable to sin, Evagrius teaches us that authentic and swift repentance is vital. Forgiveness is already ours through God's redemptive work in Christ. Thus, when we sin, all that is needed is to rely on that saving grace and turn from walking in our own direction. To repent is to stop, turn around, and find connection with God who is our salvation. Repenting is a form of salvation, for it rescues us from a destructive path. A desert elder of the time noted that the sin of lust is thwarted with confession precisely because lust thrives in hiddenness. Surely this wisdom applies more broadly to other sins as well. We are responsible for our choices, and no one gets off the hook as merely being "born depraved" when they falter.

> Nothing troubles the demon of lust more than laying bare his urgings. Nothing pleases him more than the concealment of the temptation.
>
> —anonymous desert elder, *Sayings of the Desert Fathers*

Return in Prayer

Abba Evagrius underscores that we don't appreciate forgiveness when we go about ignoring God. We snub God's love when we don't heed God or accept the grace to rectify when we rebel, disobey, or seek our own comforts apart from God. We don't find grace worthy to free us when we stay satisfied in our selfishness and pettiness. The virtues reflect the nature of God in whose image we are made. In contrast, purposeful sinfulness is a repudiation of the image of God in us.

Again and again, Evagrius advises us to return to God in prayer. It is the willingness to come before God humbly that trains us and fills us with fulfillment and peace. Knowing exactly what to say is not important, nor is imagining God in any kind of way—whether we imagine a disappointed parent, an angry Zeus holding lightning bolts, or a jolly Santa Claus who gives presents. Come to God, says Evagrius, who is beyond conception—the ground of being and reality itself.

> When you are praying, do not shape within yourself any image of the Deity, and do not let your intellect be stamped with the impress of any form: but approach the Immaterial in an immaterial manner, and then you will understand.
>
> —Abba Evagrius

Too often, we pray to God for what we want—even when we pray for the needs of others. But Abba Evagrius instructs us in a different way, saying, "Do not pray for the fulfillment of your wishes, for they may not accord with the will of God. But pray as you have been taught, saying: Thy will be done in me. Always entreat God in this way—that God's will be done. For God desires what is good and profitable for you, whereas you do not always ask for this."

Many of the elders suggest that gratitude and repentance also have a function of purgation. Using the words *holy tears*, they indicate that repentant weeping must be a part of a monastic's life. We can understand this type of lament as happening when the grief of our sin and shortcomings collides with our gratitude for being forgiven and loved. Tears pour out in catharsis when the weight of our sin and the recognition of our redemption intersect within us. It may be a foreign concept to us, though we may have experienced the "compunction of tears" (or gift of tears) at some point.

Holding Vigil

Another way of desert spirituality that now is an unfamiliar spiritual practice to many is *watching*. We might also call it *holding vigil.* Abba John explained the spiritual practice this way: "Watching means to sit in the cell and be always mindful of God. This is what is meant by, 'I was on the watch and God came to me' (Matthew 25:36)." There is eagerness and expectation in the posture of holy waiting, watching, or standing vigil. Learning that silence and watchfulness are considered forms of prayer in desert spirituality can be a liberating notion. We realize anew that those who wait on the Lord "renew their strength," as the psalms say. Patient watching in hope and trust is how we pray by *holding vigil.* From this understanding of prayer, we needn't know what to say or have all the right words to get started. Remember that silence is also prayer. Paying careful attention is prayer as well. Wholehearted attention and attunement to God are prayer.

Abba John the Small told us about keeping vigil and Abba Sisoes also spoke about gaining humility through vigil (holy waiting). Once a monk asked him, "What am I to do?" He said to him, "What you need is a great deal of silence and humility. For it is written: 'Blessed are those who wait for him' (Isaiah 30:18) for thus they are able to stand."

Join a Confessional Community

"Going it alone" spirituality, or even thinking of Christianity as any kind of solo endeavor, is a highly modern and Western phenomenon and one that deeply damages us when we try it. Even though some ascetics were hermits living in isolation, they were known to and aided by their local church communities. Each prayed for each other. The community brought supplies to them, and in turn the hermits blessed them with prayers and wisdom. Most solitaries also made time for contact with a larger community to eat and worship once each week, without fail. Even when they took vows of silence, they were rooted in something much deeper and bigger than themselves and their individual spiritual pursuit. They experienced life with the church—the people of God, one body—including members of the past, present, and future work of God, world without end. This is the rich spiritual history that belongs to all of us who admire them and try to follow their footsteps. Leaders like Abba John, Abba Moses, Amma Mary, and Amma Syncletica, and so many others worked to make their communities places where the qualities of heaven had taken root on earth.

Being part and staying part of a local community always has its challenges. As we stay with our community, however, it keeps us growing in maturity and protects us from all too quickly becoming self-serving in our interests. Too often, our consumeristic mindset dupes us into thinking that a community is something we select—like picking an item from a menu. Consequentially, that means we may feel we should discard it once the situation doesn't serve us or please us much anymore.

Church people will be difficult to be patient with sometimes. But unless there is harm happening, we should invest ourselves in our local community of believers and make a difference right where we spend the most time living. Additionally, the temptation to rely only on methods of online, virtual church means that transformational community remains remote for us. Inviting others into our lives directly begins to build in what we need with how we are designed to live interdependently. We do not mature in isolation.

"We ought to govern our souls with discretion and to remain in the community, neither following our own will nor seeking our own good," Amma Syncletica said. "We are like exiles: we have been separated from the things of this world and have given ourselves in one faith to the one Father. We need nothing of what we have left behind. There we had reputation and plenty to eat; here we have little to eat and little of everything else." Though the monastics lived with few possessions and minimal food stuffs, they had each other and everything they needed.

Spiritual director, professor, and writer Cindy S. Lee's work reminds us that modern Western impositions of domination, hierarchy, and individualism can work to harm our collective oneness. We live quite unlike the original Christian communities who began in Southwest Asia (this is just a non–Western-centered way to say "the Middle East"). Unlike the early Christians, or Christians in other cultures, our present-day Western attempts at faith community can be event-based and feel quite transactional. It can be difficult to feel cared for, grounded, and a part of the larger body of Christ in sustaining ways. When this occurs, we tend to drift into privatized spirituality. As Lee writes, "In individualistic cultures, the self is at the center, and even practices of community are determined by one's own needs." Collectivist cultures work the other way around. Their ways of knowing and practices of faith begin in a community and then move to individual expressions. Taking on the qualities of desert spirituality means thinking differently about community—outside of individualistic frameworks. The outcomes will allow us to feel more connected.

Confession is also something we should think of in the context of community, but too often we miss out on this. The way of desert spirituality reminds us that confession is not an occasional, isolated, and solo activity—because sin is not a private problem. Sin has communal consequences, and so confession and repentance must be accomplished in the context of community in order to benefit everyone. No one enjoys having conversations about their shortcomings. But an honest reckoning with reality and a willingness to change for the better are essential for our spiritual growth, health, and the sustainability of a faith community.

Additionally, for a community rooted in justice, the suffering that happens within the community must be mitigated straightaway, not glossed over. Those who have been wronged must be given a voice or else they suffer twice. Those who have done wrong also suffer without the assistance of correction. This is a context where a community expects, welcomes, and routinizes opportunities for confession, repentance, recompense, and reconciliation—not in words alone, but in sacramental and lived-out ways. Sometimes we fail to address wrongs within, or experienced by, our community simply because they have never been dealt with before—such as in cases of abuses of power, manipulation, violence, or fiscal stewardship. The desert elders show us that regularly confessing and redeeming such sinfulness is crucial to generative faith communities.

> We must direct our souls with discernment. As long as we are in the monastery, we must not seek our own will, nor follow our personal opinion, but obey our elders in the faith.
>
> —Amma Matrona

A head amma or abba and a few other elders as top assistants always oversaw a community. Problematic circumstances, whether sinful ones or interpersonal aggravations, were addressed with respect for the wholeness of community to benefit it, in order to avoid carrying forward the harm of guilt without justice.

Remember That the Cell Is the Soul

Sit in your cell, and your cell will teach you everything: This is a saying credited to Abba Moses and to a number of other desert elders. It's likely that many of them repeated and passed on this saying, because it was perfectly basic and vital to learning the ways of desert spirituality. If heeded, it was a potent form of preventive spiritual medicine. For us, the cell is our soul—the deepest part of our whole selves. It's another way to say that as we make time to sit still with God, God reveals us thoroughly to ourselves, and we are taught the most important things.

I want to underscore that it is not strict, disciplined adherence to certain practices that makes us into virtuous people. It wasn't like that for the desert dwellers either. These ways and practices don't act as a substitute for a virtuous life. Alone, they can even create the opposite effect. Accomplishing difficult practices can create conceited people who think we are better than others and begin to do harm. Regular spiritual practices are merely habits that make enacting an ongoing virtuous life more likely. The actual work of spiritual practices is to make us ready to change and be made new. It is always the struggle by fire that leads to a possibility of refinement. Let us be faithful to a life that is purified by holy fire.

> Many people living secluded lives on the mountain have perished by living like people in the world. It is better to live in a crowd and want to live a solitary life than to live a solitary life but all the time be longing for company.
>
> —Amma Matrona

Our disconnection with the presence of God, and others, shows up within us as loneliness or emptiness. We can feel estranged from our deepest selves. As this hunger is met by deeper intimacy with the Divine, we then have the reserves to meet others with more generosity. We can connect more deeply in our relationships, but also in our faith community. Instead of entering into interactions and sharing of life from a place of deficit, of neediness, and of a self-centered framework, we can retain a stable, inner calm, and centeredness as we interact with others for the benefit of the entire community. This is what spiritual maturity looks like in action.

Reflect and Respond

- What ways from the desert elders speak to you the most in this chapter?
- How might you have been trying to "go it alone" spiritually?
- What are specific ways you can built deeper connections with others?

Pray

O my Creator,
One with no beginning, no end, uncontainable,
You are holy.
I let fall away what I should not hold on to.
Help me grasp what keeps me well.
I have sinned against you, God, and others.
Others have sinned against me.
Forgive us. How deeply we need your grace.
Allow me to feel your love for me,
And take me into your embrace.
I am yours and you are mine.
Amen.

CHAPTER 11

Keeping the Elders Close

A Rule of Life

> The one who sits in solitude and is quiet has escaped from three wars: hearing, speaking and seeing: yet against one thing will they continually battle: that is, their own heart.
>
> —Antony the Great

Once we've learned about the desert spirituality of the ammas and abbas, we often can't stop thinking about them. They start to feel like kind relatives, and we long to sense them close by, guiding us amid the frenzy of life. Their ways, which can at times feel ancient or strange, also insistently beckon to us. They inspire us to imitate their devotion and renew our fervor. They make us wonder how we might seek virtuous ways, pursue intimacy with God, and find harmony with others in ever more sustaining ways.

But by this point you might also be thinking, Yes, the desert elders are fascinating and they lived faithful lives. But my life now is so loud and so busy and so complicated. Moving off to a desert community is not going to happen. Can I really emulate the spirituality of the desert abbas and ammas in meaningful ways?

While it's true that desert hermits and monastics had lives far removed from what we experience in a typical day, the human vulnerabilities that plagued them plague us too. The real test of spiritual maturity isn't whether it works on an isolated mountaintop cabin or a refreshing retreat center; it's whether we have been transformed so that our maturity plays out in regular life. Untold numbers of Christians, most of whom remain forgotten by history, found stillness and peace right in the middle of the stress and chaos of ordinary life, and many still do. They are the innumerable and unnamed ordinary saints—a grand cloud of witnesses who also cheer us on from just beyond the veil. Like us, they don't have feast days named after them, but they are no less real or inspirational.

All the desert abbas and ammas show us that one-off special insights are not what bring us spiritual maturity or peace. Through the layering of situations, struggles, and seasons, we grow more devoted, mature, and wise. The inheritance in the kingdom of heaven means possessing Christlikeness; this inheritance comes in slow disbursements that take diligence and attention to learn and receive. We accomplish this not over weeks or months but over decades—over our lifetime and even into and throughout generations. The pace is slow. Let's get accustomed to that and settle in for the long haul.

The spiritual seeds the ammas and abbas once planted in the fertile soil of seekers can still beautifully bloom now in the soil of you, more than 1,500 years later. This is how the glory of God works. You are the glory of God made manifest.

> In the beginning, there is struggle and a lot of work, but in the end, there is tranquility.
>
> —Amma Syncletica

Let's also remember that there are concrete things that can help us. We can develop, as they did, a *rule of life* to guide us in our context. A rule of life can serve as the method that sustains a desert spirituality. The word used for *rule* in the phrase *rule of life* comes from the Latin word for *trellis*—a simple structure that supports healthy growth for vines. Without a trellis, vines grow all over instead of up. For optimal growth, vines need to get off the too moist ground and into the air above, where they get more light to thrive.

A community with a rule of life sets in place a sturdy trellis. Such supports offer us better spiritual conditions than our solo efforts or haphazard formats could ever do. This was the greatest benefit for the desert-dwellers in those early communities: the communal support and the functioning structure of a rule of life.

> We who have chosen this way of life must obtain perfect temperance.
>
> —Amma Syncletica

Amma Syncletica created a rule of life in her community that lasted long after she was gone and that we can use as inspiration to create our own. Indeed, we can't finish speaking about the elders before we learn more about the life of beloved Amma

Syncletica, who has been teaching us through her many sayings already. The record of her life demonstrates a steady faithfulness that many have found beautiful and inspiring.

Amma Syncletica, Mother of the Desert Seekers

Amma Syncletica was sometimes revered as "the female counterpart to St. Antony." There is some debate about the span of her life, but it may have lasted from around 340s–420s CE. Other than Abba Antony, this beloved spiritual mother was the only other desert elder to be so esteemed as to be called *holy* while still alive. Twenty-seven of Amma Syncletica's sayings have been preserved—more than those of any other desert mother. Syncletica and Antony both gave up their wealth to live in the desert as monastics. They both had remarkable humility and wisdom, and they both amassed followers and founded monastic communities.

Amma Syncletica was born the daughter of wealthy and devout parents who moved from Macedonia to the bustling city of Alexandria, where a particularly vibrant and loving Christian community was gaining a reputation for its virtue. Her family were upper-class seafaring merchants, and she was highly educated and quite bright.

Syncletica's name means "heavenly assembly," and even in childhood, it's said that she longed for the devout life. As a young person, Syncletica had two older brothers who both died, thus leaving her with her family's riches. Her remaining sibling was a younger sister who was blind and needed her help. She eschewed the advances of suitors interested in marriage, and when her parents died, she gave away her wealth and took her sister with her to the wilderness.

At first, she kept a vow of silence and sought solitude. But soon many women who were spiritual seekers sought her to learn from her wisdom and be near her kindness. Eventually she founded a settled monastic community for women, which grew rapidly in numbers. Men sought her counsel as well.

Some reports say Amma Syncletica gave refuge and hospitality to the great and beloved Athanasius, celebrated now as one of the four Doctors of the Eastern Church, who was also the Patriarch of Alexandria. At the time there were massive tensions between the church and the state (Roman Empire), so that a few emperors and church leaders had Athanasius exiled. He was running for his life on occasions during this tumultuous period, and for more than a year, Athanasius went into hiding under her care at her community. He had good relationships with the desert monastics and spent many of his years of exile in their company at various locations. This desert period helped him do a lot of writing, including some foundational work for the momentous Christian document called the Nicene Creed.

After Syncletica's death, an account of her life called a *vita* ("life story") was written and ascribed to Athanasius, although most scholars agree this work likely came later by an anonymous writer, who may have had Athanasius's written accounts and other records from which to draw.

When Amma Syncletica was eighty-five years old, a painful malignant cancer began eating away her body. In her final three months, it destroyed her voice and disfigured her face as it festered with foul-smelling gangrene. She endured this suffering with gentle patience and encouraged her students, saying, "If illness strikes us, let us not be distressed as though physical exhaustion could prevent us from singing God's praises; for all these things are for our good and for the purification of our desires. Fasting and ascesis are enjoined on us only because of our appetites; so, if illness has blunted their edge, there is no longer any need for ascetic labors. To endure illness patiently and to send up thanksgiving to God is the greatest ascesis of all."

In her *vita* we find one of the basic texts of Orthodox Christian spirituality. It offers this salient advice to anyone involved in community. She advises, "It is dangerous for someone not formed by experience of the ascetic life to try to teach; it is as if someone whose house is unsound were to receive guests and cause them injury by the collapse of the building. It is the same in the case of someone who has not first built an interior dwelling; [they] cause loss to those who come."

Amma Syncletica's life was marked by patterns of faithfulness. Desert spirituality has a way of shaping you toward disciplined attentiveness to the movements of God. So how might we begin to imagine or implement a rule of life today? For starters, you can think of your rule of life as a trellis, as we've discussed, or perhaps as the layout of your "interior dwelling," as Amma Syncletica describes.

Stillness, Solitude, and Silence

Christians who began a life of solitude, silence, and stillness in the desert places struggled and faltered, and the same will happen for you. For Amma Syncletica and other desert seekers, living in solitude, silence, and stillness created the main inner foundation for their rule of life—the format and routine ways of living. A dedication to these things helped them create the internal environment in which other crucial spiritual practices could saturate and transform their lives. Those included prayer, vigil, labor, study, fasting, and serving others at predetermined times. Desert monastics maintained a rule of life together, agreeing to live with specific patterns and rhythms each day. This commitment helped them maintain devotion, discipline, and alignment with others. In this way they could stay true to their own calling and deepest values.

Evagrius taught that the life of stillness was about communion with God. Communion with God leads to a relinquishment of the attachments, powers, and worries common in our lives. Inner stillness was foundational to the rule of life the desert monastics lived by, and Evagrius encourages us to seek it. He said, "Do you desire, then, to embrace this life of solitude and to seek out the blessings of stillness? If so, abandon the cares of the world, and the principalities and powers that lie behind them: free yourself from attachment to material things, from domination by passions and desires, so that as a stranger to all this you may attain true stillness. For only by raising [oneself] above these things can a [person] achieve the life of stillness."

For Evagrius, a rule of life had to have the crucial components of inner silence and stillness and times of solitude, and this quality of desert spirituality should deeply influence the elements of the rule of life we fashion for ourselves.

> Begin the good work of stillness and do not listen to the enemy who urges you to go out somewhere from your cell, except in great and extreme need. Through your patience you will conquer the devil.
>
> —Amma Matrona

Amma Syncletica tells us that we don't have to flee to remote places to seek and find solitude, stillness, and silence. She tells us, "There are many who live [as hermits] in the mountains and behave as if they were in the town and they are wasting their time. It is possible to be a solitary in one's mind while living in a crowd, and it is possible for one who is a solitary to live in the crowd of their own thoughts." She would have known, as she led many hundreds in the community she founded and witnessed the myriad of journeys of a variety of seekers. Her life consisted of sorting out various complications that occur when people live together; and she also devoted large amounts of time to solitude and prayer that furthered her maturity.

> Give not your heart to that which does not satisfy your heart. If you are silent, you will possess peace wherever you live.
>
> —Abba Poeman

Amma Matrona's wisdom on inner stillness and silence is helpful, too, as we move forward and begin to sense how we will take the desert wisdom with us. She explains how stillness is a primary movement of the spiritual life. Stillness starts with noticing, maturing, and adjusting to our external obstacles. Then, silence deals with internal obstacles. Silence also includes our interior posture before God. This is enhanced through prayer, and to Amma Matrona, it is specifically by praying through the Psalms. Thus, for her there are three movements: stillness, silence, and praying through the Psalms. She also counseled that reading scripture and crying tears of remorse are also both essential to spiritual maturity.

Amma Matrona once counseled Amma Melania, saying, "Do you not know that for one who does not remain in stillness it is impossible to acquire even one virtue? How can we guard the heart when the door of the tongue is open, as well as of the ears and eyes? If you want to guard your heart and become perfected in virtues, sit, remain in silence in your cell and your cell will teach you everything."

The three prominent themes of stillness, solitude, and silence are not merely the charge for the hermit in isolation. The ammas and abbas always stress that they fuel us to do right by others when we live out qualities of virtue. This story of guidance illustrates the point:

> Abba Longinus came to Abba Lucius with three concerns. First, he said, "I want to go into exile." Abba Longinus said to him, "If you cannot control your tongue, you will not be an exile anywhere. Therefore, control your tongue here [in community], and you will be an exile." Next the student said, "I wish to fast." The Abba Longinus replied, "Isaiah said, 'If you bend your neck like a rope or a bulrush, that is not the fast I will accept; but rather, control your evil thoughts [in community]'" (Isaiah 58). Finally, Abba Lucius said to his teacher Abba Longinus, "I wish to flee from [people]." Abba Longinus replied, "If you have not first of all lived rightly with [people], you will not be able to live rightly in solitude."

Similarly, *hesychasm* is a tradition and movement that originated with the legacy of the desert elders and is claimed as heritage by Eastern and Oriental Orthodox Christians. Hesychasm can refer to inner or outer stillness and comes from a Greek word meaning stillness, rest, quiet, or silence.

In fourth- and fifth-century writings, desert fathers such as Abbas Macarius of Egypt, Evagrius, and Gregory of Nyssa used the words *hesychast* and *hesychia* frequently. The desert elders cultivated inner tranquility, and this way of being was central to their continual practice of prayer. Hesychasm involves a lifestyle with the ongoing practice of "interior silence and continual prayer."

In the Byzantine Era of the fourteenth century, *hesychasm* was more formalized as spiritual practices and meditative prayer techniques. It then became distilled and more closely identified with a prayer practice known as the Prayer of the Heart, also called the Jesus Prayer, which we learned in chapter 9. The Jesus Prayer, which is usually prayed with these words, "Lord, Jesus Christ, have mercy on me, a sinner," is also known as more broadly as *arrow prayer*—a short message sent straight to God.

Pacing Yourself

It may seem overwhelming to consider living the rest of our lives in a new sort of holiness. Little-known Abba Hyperichius offers us wisdom to pace ourselves well for this life, saying, "Praise God continually with spiritual hymns and always remain in meditation and in this way, you will be able to bear the burden of the temptations that come upon you. A traveler who is carrying a heavy load will pause from time to time and draw in deep breaths; it makes the journey easier and the burden lighter."

Abba Hyperichius mentions a kind of unflustered disposition we take up when we have the long view in mind—when we commit to a long journey of obedience and reorientation into the likeness of Christ. It's an epic trip that can, or rather will, involve periods of distress, difficulty, and tempting choices. Without keeping the praises and songs of God—and the other wisdom we've learned from the desert elders—as the meditation of our heart, it can sometimes feel too hard to continue faithfully. Let us retain such meditations and wisdom as places of oasis that serve to help us catch our breath and maintain our rhythm. This is how we put a claim on peace as we walk in the way of the Master Jesus.

We have much to learn and we adjust to a desert spirituality best when we seek wisdom and support from each other in a close-knit community committed to intimacy with God and Christlikeness. Within a world of interconnectedness, the desert seekers discerned their way using the ongoing advice of their abbas and ammas. "Their ecclesial world was still Orthodox and sacramental," says Coptic Orthodox Christian Phoebe Farag Mikhail. "They communed and they confessed, and that's what helped them take this path of asceticism with balance and humility." Together. Onward. Humbly.

Living with Love

Part of living with each other well means that we don't expel our disappointments, resentments, or irritations about others. We take them directly to God. Most of us are used to sharing news and our frustrations with other people, but the elders tell us we need to do things differently.

A student once asked Abba Poemen, "If I see my brother sin, is it right to say nothing about it?" The old man replied, "Whenever we cover our brother's sin, God will cover ours; whenever we tell people about our brother's guilt, God will do the same about ours." Abba Poemen isn't referring to hiding abuse or wrongs that tear people and communities apart. When he says "cover," he means graciously overlooking the offenses and mistakes others make that irritate you.

Don't gossip, share news, or mention your "prayer requests" about them. Don't embarrass them or seek to make them repent because something annoys you. When we create a boundary this way, we allow God to handle our frustrations instead of perpetuating acrimony. The elders teach us that surely others may be guilty of falling short, but so are we, and God overlooks it because of God's grace and love toward us. This is a beautiful lesson from desert spirituality that can be a healing salve for our context, if we let it.

Enacting Charity and Compassion

The aim of the monks' lives was not asceticism but God, and the way to God was charity. It is by becoming loving that we know God the most intimately. Through tender charity, simple hospitality, and acts of service like helping a monastic who was ill, the desert elders added meaning to their days. Their works tested whether the love of God was in them. Charity was to be total and complete. The men and women of the desert received guests in the same manner that they would receive a visit from Jesus himself. Though they normally practiced some kind of fasting, when visitors arrived, desert ascetics laid their austerity and fasting practice aside, welcomed them with joy, and ate along with them. Amma Matrona noted that charity and compassion were central to sensing the love of God within. She once said, "Whoever visits the sick, or gives consolation to the sorrowful, or comforts someone wronged, or seeks those in need, will be met by the love of God." When was the last time you felt met by the love of God? This is how it powerfully happens.

> There is no greater love than that a man lays down his life for his neighbor. When you hear someone complaining and you struggle with yourself and do not answer him back with complaints; when you are hurt and bear it patiently, not looking for revenge; then you are laying down your life for your neighbor.
>
> —Abba Poemen

Bearing Fruit and Repenting

Abba James said, "We do not only need words, for at the present time there are many words among [people]; but we need works, for this is what is required—not words that do not bear fruit." This spiritual father knew that words can be cheap. It is actions that carry the most value. The monastics often kept talking to a minimum and this helped them choose their words carefully and keep their deeds righteous. The spiritual fruit evident in our lives testifies to the love of God within us and the words we use does the same.

Let us remember, too, how the desert elders spoke about *ongoing* repentance. Temptation is normal, failure is normal, so repenting must be just as common.

> A brother asked Abba Sisoes, "I have fallen, Abba; what shall I do?" The old man said to him, "Get up again." The brother said, "I have gotten up again, but again have I fallen." The old man said, "Get up again and again."

> So the brother asked, "How many times?" The old man replied, "Until you are taken up either in virtue or in sin. For a [person] presents themself to judgment in that state in which [they are] found."

The elderly Abba Sisoes advised that we spend the shortest time possible in a wayward state. Don't waste a minute. Always be found in a state moving toward virtue, he tells us.

> Courage stands in the middle between cowardice and foolhardiness; humility in the middle between arrogance and servility. Modesty is a mean between timidity and boldness.
>
> —Abba Dorotheos

Learning Wisdom

Learning from people from another time can present challenges because we encounter so much that the ancients never did. Yet in most ways, the wisdom of the desert elders transcends time and place because it speaks to the fundamental shortcomings and temptations that we all face as human beings. Their wisdom helps us navigate difficult situations and teaches us to create habits that protect us and others. The ammas and abbas grew closer to the felt presence of a loving God mainly by thwarting distractions, temptations, and sin that diverted them from *prayer*. This may not be a way we typically think about creating ongoing intimacy with God, but consider how our love of God, a kind of gaze and gratitude toward God, can be a living prayer in itself. This mindfulness is a way of *being*, a spiritual sensitivity and tenderheartedness to the ways and will of God. It's a way of living we can begin and endeavor to continue so that we become sustained.

Amma Theodora heartens us into a fruitful, long-term, spiritually faithful life by saying, "Let us strive to enter by the narrow gate. Just as the trees, if they have not stood before the winter's storms cannot bear fruit, so it is with us; this present age is a storm and it is only through many trials and temptations that we can obtain an inheritance in the kingdom of heaven."

As we purposefully bring the desert legacy and lessons to bear on our lives, our relationships, and our walk of faith with God, we must also share these things with others who've never heard of our spiritual forebears. Their ways of bringing God into every moment can inspire us to change how we strive to live and interact with others now. Consider now, What lesson or story could you share with a friend or in your community?

Crafting a Rule of Life

As we prepare to leave these desert places, for now, let's first consider which wise teachings we can take with us and how we can put them into practice. What lessons of faith, hope, and love have we learned from our desert guides, and how might they help us approach trials, temptation, suffering, and desolation? Review the nine temptations and also reexamine the elders' quotes sprinkled all through this book. Which advice impacts you most deeply? What inspires you to live differently? Which temptations hinder you most? What do you want to change and how will you do it? Meditate on these things and bring them to God. Allow God to speak to you as you move forward. Allow God to connect you to others to share this journey.

It's not hard to create your own concrete ways and rhythms of being that echo the qualities of desert spirituality and wisdom of the ammas and abbas. Your life already has habits, patterns, and rhythms to it. As you inspect that more closely and make a list on paper, consider what you want to trim away and also what you want to attach to the trellis as you move forward. Add what nurtures you and lifts you up but also what cajoles you to be your best and connects with others in deeper ways.

A helpful way to begin is to take four or five practices or pieces of wisdom that feel meaningful to you and note how and when you will incorporate one or two of them—first in your daily life. Then add one or two that apply to your life to accomplish weekly. Take what you've decided, and note these on a desk calendar, on an app in your phone, in a file on your computer, or on a paper wall calendar you will encounter each day. Like eating, brushing your teeth, or washing up, these practices can become established routines, and in this case ones that offer spiritual hygiene and sustenance. After that, include which one or two practices you will do each month; and lastly, add one or two that will be yearly activities. Your pattern, or rule to live by, is now established. Additional resource links are available in the back of the book to help you a bit more.

To illustrate this better, let's imagine the life of a contemporary person who is seeking God and crafting a rule of life: Chris, a working professional with a family and a sizable load of responsibilities, is eager to adapt some ways of the desert elders and to figure out what habits of devotion, inspired by them, might look like in her busy contemporary life.

In a notebook, Chris delineates her preferences for a *rule of life*. First, she wants to find a time of inner silence and solitude each *day*. So she decides that while the morning tea steeps, a spiritual practice, inspired by the ammas and abbas, will happen: She prays a psalm or the Jesus Prayer. Chris also decides to pray a psalm or the Jesus Prayer during extra moments of preparation early in the day and again around ten minutes before bed. This is her daily rule.

Then, Chris prayerfully considers a practice to do weekly. In this case, she looks for a specific way of extending hospitality and humility for each *week*. Chris reaches out to care for someone in need, or gives something to someone in secret. Chris decides on a mix of ordinary and more extraordinary practices that will challenge her avarice, vainglory, and pride. Chris alternates between visiting an elderly relative, coaching a neighbor child on sports skills, and helping a neighbor get to chemo appointments. Chris doesn't post about these things on social media, or tell others about it, and over time she notices that the urge to do so isn't even there. She is thwarting a common temptation of vainglory. This is her weekly rule.

For a *monthly* practice, Chris decides to enact an ascetic practice like refraining from sweets or a meal. This happens one day per month. When Chris feels the (minor) deprivation, she remembers to be grateful, to pray, and to lean into worship. This limited fasting practice works to bring her renewed focus and more gratitude. This is her monthly rule.

Once a *year*, then, Chris decides to undertake a day-long spiritual retreat and visit a wise spiritual director. Chris finds a trained person and uses the time to find deeper inner silence and be guided in deeper listening to the holy. Chris's director asks her questions to pray about and ponder, allowing the Holy Spirit to work on those things slowly within. Chris can then pick some areas to let go and choose some goals or practices moving forward, and regroup in a year's time. This is her yearly rule. All together, these habits, practices, activities, and patterns comprise her rule of life.

In crafting her rule of life, Chris creates a visibly noted trellis of patterns and habits that interest and enrich her. They deepen her intimacy with God and challenge her without being an overwhelming burden. After a couple years, Chris will revamp what is included, as her needs change and spiritual life deepens. Similarly, you can begin to craft a rule of life, right now, that suits your needs and longings.

As you craft your own rule of life, also consider what practices renew you when you are weary and attend to those specifically. Care for your soul in your ongoing rhythms—perhaps by adding times of sabbath, deep rest, and other regenerating practices. Add ways you will richly interact with others. Consider what helps connect you more deeply with God, and include that in your rule. Perhaps being in nature, singing, or praying with others makes a difference, includes what works and what honors God. Know that such an endeavor to renew your spiritual life is infused with triumphs and setbacks as you begin. Just as the spiritual seekers in the desert were encouraged to keep at it, I encourage you now.

The hermits, hooligans, and harlots of the desert era were such a colorful bunch. They inspire us to leave behind what does not help us grow or love God, our neighbors, and ourselves more fully. They invite us to seek the kingdom of God, which is a dominion of our body, mind, and spirit, on earth as it is in heaven. Wherever we find ourselves, we can draw from their hope during struggles and their persistence to help us find our way through. They have paved a way before us, and we can follow them into our own desert places and toward our true home in God.

Final Blessing

If you've been touched by the ways and wisdom of the abbas and ammas, they will stay with you and continue to teach you. Revisit their sayings to remember what they have to tell you—and to *get a word* from them so you may live a more sustained life. Be nourished by all that they were so deeply nourished by in the desolate places. When you come to desolate places or seasons in your life, I hope you won't find those spots as fruitless and hopeless as you have before. May you, instead, find them clarifying and strengthening you with the kind of Bread only God can give you—the kind that lasts forever.

As we enact a desert spirituality that sustains us, and as we find a centered and stable divine presence of Love with us, let us remember that millions of people, now and through the millennia, have found the goodness of God the same way. In returning to these sturdy and ancient roots, we will sense greater spiritual fulfillment and interconnectedness. Remember such roots are intertwined with mystery and go deeper into the heart of God than our flights of fancy, hurt wanderings, or restless excursions ever can.

As you commit to return to the wadis of the desert again and again, to be taught by your abbas and ammas, receive this blessing:

> May the nourishment that comes from God be yours
> May you find in your desert places the abundance that can only come
> from the Source of all Goodness and Life
> May the stillness within subdue any fear and overcome any sense of isolation

May the depths you find be fertile ground and the womb of new spiritual life
May the way of simplicity, holiness, and devotion inspire you and be your contentment
May the trifles and enticements of this wanton world shackle you no more
May you nourish the relationships that bring loving mutuality and ongoing care
May you sit in your cell so it may teach you everything
Amen, and God be with you

AUTHOR'S NOTE

Note on distinctions within Christian Orthodoxy. Writer Phoebe Farag Mikhail, a Coptic Orthodox Christian, helped me better understand some essential distinctions of Eastern Orthodox and Oriental Orthodox Christians that have ethnic, racial, and doctrinal components. I will paraphrase her input here:

The Eastern Orthodox Christians are predominantly people with light skin color: Eastern European, Greek, Russian, Ukrainian, Serbian, Romanian, etc. Perhaps the only exception is the Antiochians—who came from a split during the Chalcedonian controversy in the mid-400s.

The Oriental Orthodox are predominantly people with dark skin color: Africans, Syrians, Indians, etc. Historically, there have been protests against ecumenism (and Oriental Orthodox Christians) in Greece by Eastern Orthodox monks and racial prejudice undertones are present.

The Oriental Orthodox Church is a very early branch of Christianity; it links itself to the Apostle Mark in 40 CE. It includes several churches, such as the Coptic (Egyptian), Ethiopian, Armenian, Syrian, Indian, and Eritrean churches. These churches do not accept the determinations of the Council of Chalcedon in the fifth century, because they reject the Christological definition of Chalcedon. Chalcedonian churches believe that Jesus is one person with two natures, divine and human, that are united without confusion or separation.

Note on Race. Here we must elucidate the way that racial prejudice occurs in some accounts of Abba Moses and other people. A number of stories of Moses, Athanasius, and John the Short, and some other figures, make reference to their Blackness (skin pigment), not in a merely descriptive manner, but in a derogatory manner; and other examples disparage those with dark skin while giving preference to light skin. Likewise, some of the stories of Moses (at least in the English translations I've encountered) are overtly racist, such as instances that directly infer that being Black is bad and being white is good. Some of this sentiment appears to come straight from Moses himself—such internalized racism is not surprising but is most regrettable. I refute these as inaccurate portrayals of any child of God.

It should be noted that "race" was determined as a difference based on physical appearance and began nearly a thousand years later than the life of Moses. It was also a way to justify the trans-Atlantic slave trade—though ethnic prejudice and discrimination on the basis of physical appearance was not absent in antiquity. It is clear from my research that specific ethnicities were preferred or considered superior to others, and these harmful attitudes made it to the desert setting, at times, and have lingered well into our time.

To overlook the apparent cruelty and racial harm of these stories would be remiss. Examples of prejudice like this, as well as sexist ones, are a lamentable aspect of the period that are without excuse and call for repentance. God, forgive us. May our brothers and sisters forgive us.

RESOURCES

For accessing resources mentioned in the book. Helpful and interesting extras for this book—such as images, artifacts, pilgrim tokens, maps, tools, and other resources—can be found at desert.lisadelay.com.

For finding a spiritual director. Find a spiritual director or companion online at this resource: https://www.sdicompanions.org.

For crafting a rule of life. Here are a few online resources:

- Free workbook PDF: https://practicingthewayarchives.org/unhurrying-with-a-rule-of-life/workbook
- SacredOrdinaryDays.com (resources and liturgical planner products)
- https://www.elizabethrosswrites.com (Rhythm of Life section; paid resource)
- App (paid tool) https://www.practicingtheway.org/ruleoflifebuilder

For sources for epigraphs and call-out quotations. Epigraphs and call-out quotations throughout the chapters are found in the following places:

John Cassian's Institutes
Athanasius: The Life of Antony

The Sayings of the Desert Fathers: The Alphabetical Collection

Ladder of Divine Ascent

The Matericon: Instructions of Abba Isaiah to the Honorable Nun

Amma Sarah: https://ia600203.us.archive.org/3/items/fiftyspiritualho00pseuuoft/fiftyspiritualho00pseuuoft.pdf

St. Macarius: https://bishoysblog.com/wp-content/uploads/2015/01/fifty-spiritual-homilies-st-macarius-the-great.pdf

The Evergetinos: https://www.ctosonline.org/patristic/EvCT.html

Evagrius of Pontus: The Greek Ascetical Corpus

Syncletia of Alexandria: https://www.oca.org/saints/lives/2012/01/05/100099-venerable-synkletika-of-alexandria

Amma Syncletica: https://desertspiritpress.net/2022/08/26/the-desert-mothers-amma-syncletica/

For further reading. The works listed here helped me write this work and will help you learn more or research the era more thoroughly.

Primary Works (Translations)

Evagrius:

The Praktikos (The Practice), *Gnostikos* (The Knower), *Kephalaia Gnostica* (The Gnostic Chapters), Antirrhetikos, and *Talking Back: A Monastic Handbook for Combating Demons*. Some smaller papers on *The Eight Spirits of Evil, On Thoughts, On the Vices Opposed to the Virtues, Foundations of Monastic Life* (Hypotyposis), *Exhortations to the Monks*, and *To Monks in Community* and *Exhortations to a Virgin* (Ad Monachos)

Athanasius of Alexandria: *The Life of Antony and the Letter to Marcellinus*. Robert C. Gregg (trans.) This can be downloaded from ccel.org/schaff/npnf204.html

Evergetinos: A copy can be purchased here: https://www.ctosonline.org/patristic/EvCT.html

Evagrius of Pontus: The Greek Ascetic Corpus, translated with introduction and commentary by Robert E. Sinkewicz

Important Secondary Works

The Sayings of the Desert Fathers: The Alphabetical Collection; and *Harlots of the Desert: A Study of Repentance in Early Monastic Sources* by Benedicta Ward

Dragon's Wine and Angel's Bread: Teaching of Evagrius Ponticus on Anger and Meekness by Gabriel Bunge

Balance of the Heart; Desert Spirituality for 21st Century Christians by Mother Lois Farag

The Story of the Copts: The True Story of Christianity in Egypt by Iris Habib el Masri

Practical Spirituality According to the Desert Fathers by Father Athanasius Iskander

History

The Heritage of the Stylites by G.R.H. Wright

The Story of Christianity Volumes 1 & 2 by Justo L. Gonzalez

The Desert a City: An Introduction to the Study of Egyptian and Palestinian Monasticism under the Christian Empire by Derwas J. Chitty

The Seven Deadly Sins: Their Origin in the Spiritual Teaching of Evagrius the Hermit by Angela Tilby

Lives of the Desert Fathers: Cistercian Studies Series, translated by Norman Russell

The Inner Way (Christian Classics Ethereal Library) by John Tauler

Other Important Works

The Desert Mothers: Spiritual Practices from the Women of the Wilderness by Mary C. Earle

The Wisdom of the Desert Fathers and Mothers by Henry Carrigan

The Ancient Path: Old Lessons from the Church Fathers for a New Life Today by John Talbot and Mike Aquilina

Praying with the Desert Mothers by Mary Forman OSB

Desert Daughters, Desert Sons: Rethinking the Christian Desert Tradition by Rachel Wheeler

The Forgotten Desert Mothers: Sayings, Lives and Stories of Early Christian Women by Laura Swan

The Way of the Heart: The Spirituality of the Desert Fathers and Mothers by Henri Nouwen

The Wisdom of the Desert by Thomas Merton

ACKNOWLEDGMENTS

Deep thanks to Broadleaf Books, my publisher, and to my editor, Valerie Weaver-Zercher, for another partnership and making something special for readers that I hope will be an evergreen resource. May it inspire devotion and bring glory to God!

Much gratitude to my agent, Keely Boeving, who shepherded me through the process of attempts until we landed on this. Your hard work is appreciated. Thank you.

Thank you to the talented artist Kreg Yingst who offered his four outstanding woodcuts of the desert elders for the part openers as well as the cover art. Those and many more pieces are available at kregyingst.com

A special thanks to Carmen Acevedo Butcher, who first encouraged me to take on this early Christian time period and the wise elders of it. Carmen was the person who first sang the praises of Amma Syncletica to me, which lit my fire of inspiration.

Thanks to my beta readers and encouragers: Phoebe Farag Mikhail, Lindsay O'Conner, Jessica Whittemore, and Dave Ward. Deep appreciation to friend and writer Phoebe Farag Mikhail and to Dr. Mary Farag, a faculty member at Princeton Theological Seminary, for cultural, historical, and non-Western insights that reflect Coptic Orthodox understandings. My first draft suffered from some omissions that reflected a lack of perspectives outside European or typical North American ones that can dominate the market.

And friends Cindy S. Lee, Beth Allison Barr, Karen Swallow Prior, Chuck DeGroat, Christine Valters Paintner; my financial supporters, Substack subscribers, and Patreon patrons; online listeners, readers, and other online followers; friends; dozens of kind writer compadres, church friends, and others who provided kindness or support of various kinds and are too many to name here: you have my deep gratitude.

NOTES

Listed according to page number.

Introduction

2 ***By the fifteenth century:*** "Estimated Total Number of Monasteries in Various Regions of Western Europe in Each Century between 500 and 1500 CE," Statista, https://www.statista.com/statistics/1396363/europe-medieval-monasteries-region/.

10 ***"Do not think that a demon":*** Abba Loukios and other abba sayings are located in the *Evergetinos*: https://www.ctosonline.org/patristic/EvCT.html.

11 ***"We must observe the assaults of evil spirits":*** fatherbrad1971, "The Desert Mothers: Amma Syncletica," desertspiritpress.net, August 26, 2022, https://desertspiritpress.net/2022/08/26/the-desert-mothers-amma-syncletica/.

13 ***"cracks in the heart":*** Rev. Angela Tilby spoke of Andrew Louth and logismoi in her lectures and her book *The Seven Deadly Sins: Their Origin in the Spiritual Teaching of Evagrius the Hermit*, SPCK Publishing, 2009.

Chapter 1: Antony and the Beasts

18 ***"His doctrine surely was pure and unimpeachable":*** *Athanasius: The Life of Antony*, Beloved Publishing LLC, 2014.

19 ***"This is the great work of a human":*** Benedicta Ward, *Sayings of the Desert Fathers*, Cistercian Publications, 1984.

20 ***"Here am I, Antony":*** Ibid.

20 ***"making the sign of the cross made demons run away":*** Ibid.

25 ***the elders often suggested moderation:*** Mother Lois Farag, *Balance of the Heart; Desert Spirituality for 21st Century Christians*, Cascade Books, 2012.

30 ***These degrees are temperance, sufficiency, and satiety:*** Gregory of Sinai, *St. Nicodemos of the Holy Mountain, A Handbook of Spiritual Counsel*, Paulist Press, 1988.

Chapter 2: There's Something About Mary

41 ***"Whether it's sexual lust":*** Personal correspondence with author, Phoebe Farag Mikhail, January 2025.

41 ***Mary, the grazing hermit:*** Story of Mary comes from "Saint Mary of Egypt," Catholic Saints, Newman Connection, https://www.newmanministry.com/saints/saint-mary-of-egypt.

47 ***an average of eighteen minutes:*** TrueAlly Team, "How Many People Watch Porn?" TrueAlly, May 29, 2024, https://trueally.app/blog/how-many-people-watch-porn-2024-stats-trends/.

52 ***"I visited Abba Macarius the Younger":*** "A Word from Evagrius," https://www.evagrius.net/2013/05/the-eight-patterns-lust.html.

53 ***"To say that God turns away":*** Ward, *Sayings of the Desert Fathers.*

Chapter 3: Ladies of the Realm

67 ***"Amma Paula did when she helped Jerome":*** Women and the vulgate: A. H. Johns, "Woman's Work in Bible Study and Translation," Catholic Culture, https://www.catholicculture.org/culture/library/view.cfm?recnum=2945.

71 ***"You have achieved a small victory":*** *The Matericon: Instructions of Abba Isaiah to the Honorable Nun,* St. Paisium Serbian Orthodox Monastery, 2001.

73 ***92 million tons of unused garments:*** Martina Igini, "10 Concerning Fast Fashion Waste Statistics," Earth.org, August 21, 2023, accessed December 2024, https://earth.org/statistics-about-fast-fashion-waste/.

73 ***poorer countries like Chile, Ghana, and Kenya:*** Manuel Bojorquez and Kery Breen, "Inside the Landfill of Fast-Fashion: 'These Clothes Don't Even Come from Here,'" *CBS News*, December 16, 2023, accessed February 2025, https://www.cbsnews.com/news/inside-the-landfill-of-fast-fashion-chile/.

73 ***31.7 milllion kilos:*** Ibid.

73 ***368 metric tons each year:*** Tony R. Walker, "(Micro)plastics and the UN Sustainable Development Goals," *Green and Sustainable Chemistry* 30 (August 2021), accessed February 2025, https://www.sciencedirect.com/science/article/pii/S2452223621000535.

73 ***sea birds contain plastic debris in their bodies:*** Associated Press, "Up to 90% of Seabirds Have Plastic in Their Guts, Study Finds," *The Guardian*, September 1, 2015, accessed February 2025, https://www.theguardian.com/environment/2015/sep/01/up-to-90-of-seabirds-have-plastic-in-their-guts-study-finds.

Chapter 4: Moses the Strong

88 ***"My sins run out behind me":*** "Sayings of the Desert Fathers," Quies, http://www.quies.org/quies_pclc_sayings_desertfathers.php

90 ***"then our body senses them also":*** Lisa Feldman Barrett, *How Emotions are Made: The Secret Life of the Brain*, Mariner Books, 2018.

95 ***Abba Evagrius called wrath "dragon's wine":*** Evagrius on Dragon's Wine from Gabriel Bunge, *Dragon's Wine and Angel's Bread: Teaching of Evagrius Ponticus on Anger and Meekness*, St Vladimirs Seminary Pr, 2009.

95 ***Abba Evagrius calls "angel's bread":*** Ibid.

98 ***"One should not be able to fool":*** "Amma Syncletica of Alexandria Part 1," Wind Ministries, accessed November 2024, https://www.windministries.ca/blog/amma-theodora?rq=amma%20theodora.

102 ***"This is what it means":*** Ward, *Sayings of the Desert Fathers.*

Chapter 5: Wee Abba John

106 ***"Who is this John":*** "Sayings of the Desert Fathers."

107 ***"Therefore, get up early":*** Abba John the Dwarf: ibid.

107 ***"Persevere in keeping vigil":*** accessed November 2024, https://media.ancientfaith.com/sotd/11_09_john_pc.mp3.

109 ***"If you find yourself in a monastery":*** "A Selection of the Sayings of Amma Syncletica," The Carmelite Centre Melbourne, https://www.thecarmelitecentremelbourne.org/wp-content/uploads/Sayings-of-Amma-Syncletica.pdf.

110 ***"Acedia has come so far":*** Kathleen Norris, *Acedia & Me: A Marriage, Monks, and a Writer's Life*, Penguin Publishing Group, 2010.

112 ***"rely on [our] independence":*** Jean-Charles Nault on Acedia and nihilism: John-Charles Nault, "Acedia: Enemy of Spiritual Joy," *Communio* 31 (Summer 2004), https://www.communio-icr.com/files/Nault31-2.pdf; Jean-Charles Nault, *The Noonday Devil*, Ignatius Press, 2015.

113 ***"[acedia] also sends us backward":*** Norris, *Acedia & Me*.

113 ***"One day when I was suffering":*** "Sayings of the Desert Fathers," Quies, https://www.quies.org/quies_pclc_sayings_desertfathers.php.

115 ***"Trust the original desire":*** "Amma Theodora," Wind Ministries, accessed November 2024, https://www.windministries.ca/blog/amma-theodora?rq=amma%20theodora.

116 ***"A house is not built":*** https://media.ancientfaith.com/sotd/11_09_john_pc.mp3.

Chapter 6: Antony's Successor

120 ***"There is grief that is useful":*** "A Selection of the Sayings of Amma Syncletica," The Carmelite Centre Melbourne, https://www.thecarmelitecentremelbourne.org/wp-content/uploads/Sayings-of-Amma-Syncletica.pdf.

121 ***position of village cleric:*** The story of Macarius can be found at "About," St. Macarius the Great of Egypt, The Orthodox Monastery of St. Marcarius the Great of Egypt, https://www.stmacariusoca.org/about/st-macarius-the-great-of-egypt/.

122 ***at just thirty years old:*** "Venerable Macarius the Great of Egypt," Orthodox Church in America, https://www.oca.org/saints/lives/2017/01/19/100226-venerable-macarius-the-great-of-egypt.

125 ***"In truth, the Lord seeks":*** Ibid.

125 ***concern about the lives and virtues of others:*** D. Christie and E. Douglas, "Evagrius on Sadness," *Theological Studies Faculty Works* (2009): 102. https://www.proquest.com/docview/212867075?sourcetype=Scholarly%20Journals.

127 ***"this spirit must be cast out":*** Ward, *Sayings of the Desert Fathers.*

129 ***"no mere feeling":*** Peter Kreeft: https://www.kofc.org/en//index.html (resource on vices and virtues).

130 ***"Say to God, 'Lord, help!'":*** "Venerable Macarius the Great of Egypt," Orthodox Church in America, https://www.oca.org/saints/lives/2017/01/19/100226-venerable-macarius-the-great-of-egypt.

Chapter 7: Pillars of the Community

135 ***A desert-dwelling ascetic:*** David Blaine inspired by St. Simeon: Glen David Gould, "Making a Spectacle of Himself," *The New York Times Magazine*, May 19, 2002, https://www.nytimes.com/2002/05/19/magazine/making-a-spectacle-of-himself.html.

137 ***His feast day is celebrated on September 1:*** Story and information for Simeon the Stylite: Georgia Frank, "Traveling Stylites? Rethinking the Pillar Saint's *Stasis* in the Christian East," Open Edition Books, https://books.openedition.org/efr/4305?lang=en#ftn1; Lukas Amadeus Schachner, "The Archaeology of the Stylite," https://www.academia.edu/91267705/The_Archaeology_Of_The_Stylite; "Venerable Simeon Stylites the Younger of Wonderful Mountain," Orthodox Church in America, https://www.oca.org/saints/lives/2021/05/24/101502-venerable-simeon-stylites-the-younger-of-wonderful-mountain.

139 ***to argue theological differences:*** Roger Collins, *Early Medieval Europe, 300–1000*, Bloomsbury, Red Globe Press, 2010.

139 ***Lil' Symeon's father died in an earthquake:*** Stylite information from G.R.H. Wright, "The Heritage of the Stylites," *Australian Journal of Biblical Archaeology* 1, no. 3, (1970): 206–207.
140 ***a traveler walking the five- or six-hour route:*** Ibid.
147 ***If I were to pray to God:*** "Amma Theodora."

Chapter 8: A Twist of Spite

154 ***From envy are born hatred:*** Gregory the Great, Moralia, https://www.lectionarycentral.com/GregoryMoralia/Book01.html.
157 ***A note of rivalry:*** John Wortley article: "The Spirit of Rivalry in Early Christian Monachism," 1992, https://grbs.library.duke.edu/index.php/grbs/article/download/3551/5713/15609.
158 ***Abba Ammoun asked Abba Sisoes:*** Michael Centore, *From Ammoun to Sisoes: A Path through the* Evergetinos, 2015. https://themarginaliareview.com/ammoun-sisoes-path-evergetinos-michael-centore/ https://www.ctosonline.org/patristic/EvCT.html.
159 ***At the moment we cover up:*** "Life and Sayings of Holy Abba Poemen the Great," Orthodox Christianity Then and Now, August 27, 2016, https://www.johnsanidopoulos.com/2016/08/the-life-and-sayings-of-holy-abba_27.html.
159 ***"frustrated self-exaltation":*** Carol Ruvoto, "Envy and Kindness," *Tabletalk*, May 2008.
162 ***But what a gnawing worm of the soul:*** Cyprian of Carthage, Tristise 10, https://www.newadvent.org/fathers/050710.htm#:~:text=10.,the%20same%20shall%20be%20great.
164 ***Once, when a particular brother had sinned:*** "Abba Longinus the Great," Wind Ministries, accessed November 2024, https://www.windministries.ca/blog/abba-longinus-great.

Chapter 9: The Final Delusion

168 ***which determined the Nicene Creed among other things:*** Palladius, *Lausiac History* https://www.tertullian.org/fathers/palladius_lausiac_02_text.htm.

170 ***Abba Macarius said to me:*** (Evagrius asks Macarius) Tim Vivian, trans., *St. Maccarius the Spirit Bearer: Coptic Texts Relating to Saint Macarius the Great*, St Vladimir's Seminary Press, 2004.

171 ***"visions of mobs of demons in the air":*** *The Praktikos, Evagrius* http://www.ldysinger.com/Evagrius/01_Prak/00a_start.htm.

172 ***"As long as we are in the monastery":*** "A Selection of the Sayings of Amma Syncletica," The Carmelite Centre Melbourne, https://www.thecarmelitecentremelbourne.org/wp-content/uploads/Sayings-of-Amma-Syncletica.pdf.

174 ***"with accomplished and ascetic monastics":*** Ibid.

175 ***"Every time a thought of":*** Ward, *Sayings of the Desert Fathers.*

177 ***An unknown-to-us desert abba:*** Ibid.

Chapter 10: Intimacy with God

185 ***This community accepted women of any social class:*** Laura Swan, *Forgotten Desert Mothers: Sayings, Lives, and Stories of Early Christian Women*, Paulist Press, 2022.

188 ***"Do not pray for the fulfillment":*** "On Prayer," Evagrius, https://static1.squarespace.com/static/5f23bfdbdc63bd117de1a77f/t/60d36b464259324d442e5432/1624468298689/Evagrius+-+On+Prayer.pdf.

189 ***"Watching means to sit":*** Ward, *Sayings of the Desert Fathers.*

189 ***"What you need is":*** Ibid.

191 ***"We ought to govern our souls":*** "A Selection of the Sayings of Amma Syncletica."

191 ***"In individualistic cultures":*** *Cindy S. Lee, Our Unforming: De-Westernizing Spiritual Formation*, Fortress Press, 2022. (Lee continues expounding on this in her next book: *Contemplative Witnessing: BIPOC-Centered Spiritual Direction*, Fortress Press, 2025.)

Chapter 11: Keeping the Elders Close

204 ***"There are many who":*** *The Matericon: Instructions of Abba Isaiah to the Honorable Nun*, St. Paisium Serbian Orthodox Monastery, 2001.

205 ***Abba Longinus came to Abba Lucius:*** Ward, *Sayings of the Desert Fathers.*

206 ***"interior silence and continual prayer":*** Saint Nikodemos of the Holy Mountain, Nun Christina, et al., *Philokalia,* Virgin Mary of Australia and Oceania, 2024.

206 ***"Praise God continually with spiritual hymns":*** Ward, *Sayings of the Desert Fathers.*

207 ***"Their ecclesial world was":*** Personal correspondence with Phoebe Farag Mikhail, January 2025.

208 ***"If I see my brother sin":*** Ward, *Sayings of the Desert Fathers.*

209 ***"We do not only need words":*** Ibid.

210 ***A brother asked Abba Sisoes:*** Ibid.

211 ***"Let us strive to enter by the narrow gate":*** Ibid.